2nd Edition

Music in
Secondary Schools

IRA C. SINGLETON
Formerly of the University of Cincinnati

SIMON V. ANDERSON
University of Cincinnati

ALLYN AND BACON, INC. • BOSTON

2nd Edition

MT
3
.U5
S48
1969

Preface

This book deals with music teaching in the junior and senior high schools. Its objectives are twofold. First—and this is sometimes neglected in methods books or, not infrequently, is presented only by inference—it aspires to examine the sociomusical substance of the music educator's professional commitment, and to dissect the teaching-learning act through which this professional commitment is fulfilled. Second, it aims to present specific recommendations for efficient and effective instructional procedures which will bring consistent and sustained precision to the music educator's daily work.

Thoroughly reconstructed, this second edition derives from the original manuscript of the same title published in 1963. The original has been completely rewritten in the direction of its readers' suggestions. Part I, "Music Education Today," has been reworked to account for recent developments in the American adolescent's musical subculture. Part II, "The General Music Class," has been reorganized to lay emphasis on two major responsibilities—The Development of Music Skills (Chapter 3) and The Development of Refined Perception (Chapter 4).

Part III of the first edition, "The Vocal Program," and Part IV, "The Instrumental Program," have been combined to consider circumstances that are common to both programs. Finally, the professional issues discussed in Part V of the original, "A Philosophy of Music Education," have been extracted, the answers to the questions reworded, and the concepts assigned to new locations in the revised edition—by and large, to Chapter 1 and to Chapter 10.

It must be emphasized that there is no one best method for teaching music. The variables are simply too numerous and wide. There is, however, one best approach to teaching music—a "professional approach." In music education "a professional approach" permits two choices. A music teacher may think of himself as a professional educator whose special field of work is music, or he may think of himself as a professional musician whose special field of work is public school instruction.

Generally speaking, it is the approach of a professional musician whose special field of work is public school instruction that will bring the greater breadth and depth to music programs in the schools and will, in the final analysis, bring the greater educational dividends to society. Moreover, this approach puts the music educator's work in proper context; that is, he must eventually answer to the music profession-at-large for the real significance of his labor.

What labor of "real significance" does the profession-at-large expect from the music educator? It expects the same kind of creative labor that is expected of other specialists in the profession: from the musicologist, a definitive treatise; from the performer, an unforgetable performance; from the composer, a permanent addition to the literature. From the music educator it expects an enlightened community—a perceptive, knowledgeable public, generously endowed and vigorously involved in the music of its heritage.

ACKNOWLEDGMENTS

The authors are grateful to the following individuals for their cooperation during the preparation of the original edition of this book.

Irvin Cooper, The Florida State University, Tallahassee, Fla., for information concerning vocal teaching.

Damon D. Holton, Director of Music, Norristown, Penn., for suggestions concerning instrumental music.

James E. Richards, Head, Music Department, East Texas State College, Commerce, Tex., for many valuable suggestions concerning choral music.

Robert L. Garretson, University of Cincinnati, Ohio, for reading the manuscript and offering numerous suggestions for its improvement.

Vera Freid of the Cincinnati Public Schools, James E. Richards of East Texas State College, and R. Stanwood Weeks of the Philip Lesly Company for assistance in securing photographs.

The authors are indebted to the following publishers for permission to refer to copyrighted materials in the original edition of this book.

Abrahams Magazine Service, Inc., New York, N. Y.

Allyn and Bacon, Inc., Boston, Mass.

American Journal of Psychology, Austin, Tex.

Carl Fischer, Inc., New York, N. Y.

The Macmillan Company, New York, N. Y.

Music Educators National Conference, Washington, D. C.

National Education Association, Washington, D. C.

Prentice-Hall, Inc., Englewood Cliffs, N. J.

Theodore Presser Company, Bryn Mawr, Penn.

Schmitt, Hall and McCreary Company, Minneapolis, Minn.

Summy-Birchard Company, Evanston, Ill.

United States Office of Education, Washington, D. C.

Thanks are due to many other persons—teachers, friends, colleagues, and students—whose influence helped to shape the opinions of the authors. Many of these associations are years in the past, and the specific ideas they contributed are no longer identifiable. The authors wish to express their sincere gratitude, nevertheless, to all these persons without whose help, direct or indirect, the original book and this revised edition would not have been possible.

IRA C. SINGLETON
SIMON V. ANDERSON

Contents

PART **III**

Performing Organizations

PART **IV**

Instructional Tools, Techniques, and Materials

PART *1*

Music Education Today

CHAPTER 1

The Profession

M usic education, as a profession, has its ancestry in the singing schools of the early American colonists. Nearly all characteristic features of the singing school linger yet today, in one form or another, in the field of music education. What was the singing school? What were the conditions of its development and the manner of its operation? The answers to these historical questions hold special significance for all who aspire to enter the music education profession today.

HISTORICAL ROOTS

The singing school was born in the early decades of the eighteenth century, and by 1750 was firmly established in the fabric of colonial American society. A singing school began with the arrival of a singing master in town. He recruited a number of pupils, trained them in weekly or semiweekly classes for a month or two, and concluded his visit with a concert. The local minister was often called upon to deliver a special sermon; thus, the final concert was known as a "singing lecture."

The singing master usually brought his own instruction books with him to sell. In these tunebooks the rudiments of musical notation were explained, and several psalm tunes, hymns, fuging tunes, anthems, and miscellaneous pieces were printed. This body of relatively unsophisticated music was a kind of all-purpose repertory. It was the congregational music, the secular folk music, the sacred art music, the community-singing material, the educational music of its time.

The singing master was passionately committed to the development of new and better methods of teaching the art of music to his students. His methods were "new" and "plain" and "easy." He borrowed generously from European systems and sources, offering whatever bits and clusters of teaching techniques would do the job he had set out to do. He also developed his own special American techniques—the shape-note system, for example—and, generally, adapted any and all material to his own personal manner of teaching.

In addition to these musical and educational services, the singing school served as a center of social activities during its visit to town, and the singing masters made it explicitly known that their schools would provide innocent recreational diversion for the young folks in the area.

The singing school movement reached its peak in the first half of the nineteenth century when the entire operation—recreational function, educational goals, all-purpose musical repertory, eclectic methodology, and all—slipped quietly into the framework of public institutional education. Lowell Mason, a singing master, experimented with the teaching of vocal music in the Hawes School in South Boston in 1837, the same year music was introduced in the schools of Buffalo, New York. The following year the Boston school board voted to hire a teacher of vocal music for the public schools in the city. During the next few years, between 1840 and 1852, music was introduced in many other cities—Pittsburgh, Louisville, Washington, D.C., Cincinnati, Chicago, Cleveland, San Francisco, St. Louis, Philadelphia, and New York. At this point, music had gained a strong foothold in the public grammar schools, but had not found its way into the elementary schools or the public high schools. It remained for Luther Whiting Mason to introduce music in the primary grades of the Cincinnati schools in 1857. Seven years later, Mason was in Boston organizing an elementary school music program. This was followed by the introduction of music into a Boston high school in 1869, and by provisions for music in all Boston high schools in 1872.

Despite this seemingly rapid progress, it was reported in 1886 by the United States Commissioner of Education that music was being taught regularly in fewer than 250 school systems. Perhaps this was the turning point. During the next three years the number of schools employing music teachers increased by one third. By 1899 the high school in Cambridge, Massachusetts, had expanded its music curriculum to include harmony, counterpoint, and melody writing.

A further step was taken by the New England Education League during its 1902 conference devoted to the secondary school music curriculum. This group recommended a music program extending through all four high school years and including five hours of music each week, a program endorsed by the National Education Association and by the Music Teachers National Association in 1904. Further endorsement of public school music was offered by the New England College Entrance Board and by the Middle States Association through a 1906 decision to include music in the list of subjects granted college entrance credit.

Perhaps as a result of these advancements, a music committee was among those organized by the National Education Association in 1912 to study the entire process of secondary education. The 1913 report of this committee suggested a program including ensemble singing, chorus practice, music appreciation, harmony, orchestra, and credit for applied music studied under private teachers.[1]

Instrumental music came into the public educational system in a little different manner, and, prior to World War I, it appears to have played only an incidental role in music education. School orchestras were formed in a few cities betwen 1890 and 1900, including Wichita, Kansas, Richmond and Indianapolis, Indiana, and Hartford and New London, Connecticut. These instrumental groups were informal organizations rather than products of established instrumental programs.

Los Angeles began an organized program of instrumental music by forming an orchestral department for the public schools in 1910. Violin classes were formed in the Boston public schools a year later. Other cities followed these examples until, in 1915, many were able to show considerable progress—Joliet, Illinois, with the beginnings of a band program, Kansas City with forty orchestras in elementary schools, and Oakland, California, with twenty-nine orchestras and an equal number of bands, all in elementary schools.[2] An outstanding example of the growing importance of instrumental music was the appointment in 1918 of Joseph E. Maddy to the position of Supervisor of Instrumental Music in Rochester, New York, possibly the first such position in any public school system.

During its infancy, public school instrumental music was concerned chiefly with the development of orchestras. Bands were few in number. They did not become a factor in instrumental music programs until after 1920, possibly because of the interest stimulated by military bands during

[1]Peter W. Dykema and Karl W. Gehrkens, *The Teaching and Administration of High School Music*. Boston: C. C. Birchard and Co., 1941, p. 6. For the final report of the committee referred to by Dykema and Gehrkens, see *Music in Secondary Schools: A Report of the Commission on the Reorganization of Secondary Education*, prepared by Will Earhart and Osbourne McConathy. Bureau of Education Bulletin No. 49. Washington, D. C.: Government Printing Office, 1918, the full monograph, 37 pages.

[2]Theodore F. Normann, *Instrumental Music in the Public Schools*. Philadelphia: Oliver Ditson Co., 1939, p. 14.

World War I and by the large number of men who utilized their military-band training by teaching in the public schools after their release from military service. Further stimulation was provided by instrument manufacturers who sponsored band contests, the first national contest being held in Chicago in 1923, the first state contests in 1924. These contests aroused interest among music educators who saw their inherent possibilities for stimulating the expansion of instrumental music. As a result, a national school band contest was sponsored in 1926 by the Committee on Instrumental Affairs of the Music Supervisors National Conference.

In the same year, the first National High School Orchestra played in Detroit for the Music Supervisors National Conference. This group of 246 players representing thirty-four states prompted much favorable comment. In the following year a similar orchestra played in Dallas, Texas, for a meeting of the National Education Association. The favorable impression on this important organization may have been another turning point, for instrumental music developed rapidly during the years that followed. The National Music Camp was founded at Interlochen, Michigan, in 1928. The first national school orchestra contest was held in 1929 in Mason City, Iowa. State band contests grew until, in 1932, contests in which 1050 bands participated were held in forty-four states.[3]

In the next ten years, to the beginning of World War II, instrumental music continued its growth until many communities boasted a high school band, an organized program of instrument classes or lessons in the elementary school, junior high school classes and ensembles, and a varied and active high school instrumental program. Instrumental music had at this time reached a stage of advanced development, a status which has not been markedly changed in the ensuing years.

The music education profession in the United States today is rooted in the successes of the past. Its history is relatively short. The vocal music program is only a little more than one hundred years old. The instrumental program began as recently as this century, and large forward strides have been made since World War I. Music education today finds its way into almost every community and every school, achieving results of astonishing quality and providing a strong foundation for the gradually increasing music interests of the adult population. With this heritage of achievements wrought by pioneers in music education, today's music teacher can be not only proud of his profession, but strengthened in his determination to push even further toward the goal of music edu-

---

[3]Gerald R. Prescott and Lawrence W. Chidester, *Getting Results with School Bands.* Minneapolis, Minn.: Paul A. Schmitt Music Co., 1938, p. 9. Used by permission of Schmitt, Hall & McCreary Co.

cation—a society in which every individual is able to turn to music for the unique and deep satisfactions it can give.

GOALS AND RESPONSIBILITIES

A music educator assumes the goals and responsibilities of his profession. He makes a threefold professional commitment: (1) to perpetuate Western art music (a term, incidentally, which school children should be taught to use rather than "classical" music), (2) to develop in the general student populace a capacity for self-improvement in music, and (3) to provide for the especially talented and ambitious youngsters a reasonable preprofessional foundation in the art of music. The last item seems to be taking care of itself in America. College professors' lamentations notwithstanding, the freshman music major is today better informed and technically more proficient than ever before. The summer music camps throughout the nation are crowded with bright, aggressive, and talented young musicians, many of whom will go to college on full scholarship monies. Many of these youngsters have had private lessons, to be sure, but there are considerable numbers who have not, who have learned all they know about music from the public music educators in their communities. These boys and girls are the quality product of the public school music profession, and they stand in strong testimony to the good work being done in many of the public schools of the nation.

A more demanding responsibility, from a sociomusical standpoint, is the music education of the general populace of the land, the youngsters whose formal musical training terminates with the girls' glee club or the concert band. An even more demanding responsibility is the music education of the remaining segment of the general populace, the students whose formal music training terminates with the general music class of their junior high school years. Unless these young people are taught the things that lead to self-education in musical matters, their command of music will always be just about what it was when they concluded their formal training. This prospect is none too comforting.

The overriding social-educational goal of the profession, therefore, must be to develop in the general populace a capacity for self-improvement in music.

The whole purpose is, after all, to do something that would not get done as well on its own—to perpetuate Western art music. If music teachers merely do things that are readily and well done elsewhere, then society should immediately question the validity of the whole operation. If the music teacher takes the youngsters no deeper into Western art music than society-at-large takes them, then the enormous public expenditures of the public school music departments are not at all justified.

Specifically, for example, high school choir directors should take their students much deeper into the music than do the directors of the choirs of the local religious groups. High school band directors should do more than rehearse and perform the readily available and immediately appealing band music on the market. The directors of the village bands, industrial bands, lodge bands, and smaller military bands did that in their day. Today's "bandmaster," the director of the instrumental music in the public schools, should go beyond what society might provide for itself. He should—after he has met the very real social and recreational needs of his community: the marching band, the pep band, the large concert band—organize and direct a sophisticated and highly selective wind ensemble, a number of woodwind quintets, and all manner of large and small chamber ensembles.

Most important of all, the high school instrumental director should establish a string program at the earliest reasonable date. With sincere respect for the magnificent achievements of bandmasters in the public schools, the fact remains that the repository for the most significant utterances in the history of Western art music is the orchestra. To carry its responsibility to fulfillment, every department of instrumental music in a school system of sufficient size should aspire to the establishment of a full-blown symphony orchestra in the high school.

Just a decade or so ago, this aspiration might have been a little idealistic, but the enormous growth of municipal orchestras throughout the country in recent years indicates that America is ready. The public school director of instrumental music should take the lead.

If a new music teacher keeps his professional commitment firmly in mind, he will have a kind of built-in frame of reference for his day-to-day activities and a long-range goal for his career development. A great many major and minor issues fall into proper perspective if the new teacher establishes some notion of his place and function in the sociomusical life of the land.

PRINCIPLES OF TEACHING MUSIC

For all its bewildering complexity and magnificent diversity, music teaching is easily defined: it is the art of effecting change in musical behavior. It is, simply, the systematic application of instructional procedures which alter the way people produce or consume music. Easy to say. Nearly impossible to do with full and predictable consistency.

The problem is essentially this. Teaching is such an intensely personal art, and so many variables are always involved, that specious principles of teaching which read so well in methods books often provide very little of real utility in the immediate give-and-take of classroom instruction.

"Proceed from the known to the unknown," for example, gets academic endorsement by all, as it should. But it really provides very little solid ground for the beginning teacher because he needs many years of experience before he can readily discern "the known" in his pupils, and he needs many years of experience before he can feel confident that he is really presenting the "unknown" with any precision and clarity. Likewise with rules about "whole" and "part" learning. Even the educationists battle furiously, here. A new teacher can hardly be expected to apply a rule based on an area of such wide-open controversy. Besides, a new teacher is in no position, early in his career, to determine what is a "whole" or what is a "part" in the minds of even his average students, much less his slow and quick students.

"Effective teaching requires maximum student interest." "All information must be related to the student in a meaningful way." These and similar principles of teaching appear again and again in methods books. They should. They are perfectly reasonable statements. They do not, however, carry the beginning teacher very far beyond where his good common sense would have carried him.

Does this mean that there are no exalted principles of teaching that might bring focus to a new teacher's scattered energies while he learns his trade? At the risk of pontifical generalization, the following two principles are submitted: (1) teach open-ended, generative, primary concepts, and (2) teach these same concepts over and over again at progressive levels of increasing complexity and sophistication.

Same old stuff? No. These principles are easier to apply. A few examples will illustrate. Teach open-ended, generative, primary concepts. Do not tell the orchestra, "Get louder in measure five, please." Tell them, "The phrase reaches its peak in measure five, and we must build to our highest level of sound there to make it convincing." Do not tell the senior band, "Shorter on that sixteenth note, please." Tell them, "We usually lead to the longer notes; drive through the sixteenth note rather quickly so that the momentum of your delivery carries to the half note which follows."

Do not tell the sopranos, "You are flat on the B-natural." Tell them, "Lift the B-natural, please. It is what we call a 'leading tone,' and it should do just that—'lead' into its point of rest which is nearly always 'home plate,' the tonic." Do not tell the junior band, "Softer, softer in measures seven and eight." Tell them, "Shape your phrases, please. This phrase should taper off gently at its conclusion in measures seven and eight."

Teach the same generative concepts over and over again at progressive levels of increasing complexity and sophistication. Tell the seventh-grade girls, "Try to sound like the girl on each side of you, please; do not let your voice 'wobble.'" When they are ninth-grade girls, "Try to match sounds, girls, and let us keep the voices free of vibrato." When they are eleventh-grade girls, "Blend, ladies, blend. No vibrato, please." When they are college freshmen, "Bring the 'e' in 'Amen' forward a bit, ladies. It is much too dark. No vibrato, please."

Generally speaking, then, do not teach for terminal results—"Forte, please"; rather, teach for conceptual development—"The phrase must build here, please." With a little patience and good-natured perseverance, the conceptual seeds thus planted will germinate and grow with remarkable speed and assuredness.

PRIMARY AND SECONDARY PROFESSIONAL ATTRIBUTES

Music teaching is an art, and no amount of college study will ensure proficiency in the practice of the art. No minimum requirement in theory, or applied music, or music history, or child psychology, or public school methodology, or functional piano—none of these will guarantee even competency. As in all human endeavors, there are people who seem to have all the professional credentials, but their work never really satisfies or, at least, never rises above the commonplace. Others seem to have precious few of the credentials, and their work is consistently high level and often truly inspiring.

It would seem to follow, then, that the accepted credentials—the music teacher's professional equipment: his knowledge and proficiency in the art—are not the only point of reference for predicting and judging competence. Yes. It happens often, often enough to warrant serious attention by the entire profession: a new music teacher with barely adequate professional equipment develops into a first-rate music teacher, while another new music teacher with superb professional equipment turns out to be a dismal failure in the public classroom.

Does this mean that a bad musician can be a first-rate music teacher? No, indeed. Not at all. No more than a tricycle can be a tricycle without three wheels. Without three wheels it is something else. Without certain musical equipment a music teacher becomes something else. He becomes a social worker, or a guidance counselor, or a parent substitute, or something equally honorable and helpful to his students, but not a music teacher in the full sense of the term. For this reason, music education departments and state departments of education throughout the nation demand evidence of minimum study in various areas of the musical discipline. They know full well they cannot legislate competency, but they want to be certain that the vehicles going on the market are at least designed in the manner of tricycles, with the expected three wheels.

The analogy will serve a bit further. As a tricycle needs, by definition, three wheels, a music teacher needs, by definition, three areas of preparation, three primary attributes.

First, applied music. No one can hope to train others to produce music if he has never made a serious effort to train himself to produce music. He may have been struck down by physical limitations, psychological blocks, financial pressures, bad early training, or whatever, but nearly every good music teacher has been or is a serious student of the art of producing music.

Second, historical and theoretical foundations. No one can hope to struggle with the problems of stylistic authenticity—and this is the crux of the whole art, for all music stands or falls on its own organic logic—without some insight into the historical and theoretical determinants of style. The public schools have been accused of every conceivable musical sin, except their most serious sin, insufficient concern for stylistic honesty. Especially in the large ensembles, a certain grey uniformity creeps into the delivery of a good bit of all the music performed each year.

Third, instructional techniques. No one can teach music unless he can somehow get the pupil to understand which aspect of the musical behavior of the moment is to be changed, the direction and extent of change desired, and the reason for the change. All the methods classes, books, clinics, workshops, seminars, student teaching assignments, observation logs, and the rest are aimed at this area of preparation. In general, outside and inside the profession, methodology is given more attention than it deserves.

There seems to be no correlation, oddly enough, between greater or lesser preparation in the areas of the above three primary attributes and greater or lesser effectiveness in the music classroom. By and large, the better the musician, the better the teacher. Let no one be deceived. Let no one deceive himself. There seem to be outside factors, though, that figure in the effectiveness of a music educator's work. And the best, the really effective and productive music teachers seem to have the following traits or secondary attributes in common.

First, the best music teachers seem to have a kind of missionary zeal for the job at hand. They have a passionate conviction that their students' present musical behavior should be changed, that it simply must be changed. Moreover, they believe it really can be changed. A surprising number of fine musicians, music teachers among them, incidentally, still cling to rather conservative notions about the gifted few as opposed to the not-so-gifted many. The best music teachers have almost blind faith that the not-so-gifted many can be brought to very high levels of sophistication in their musical behavior.

Second, the best music teachers bring a visionary mind to the job. It need not be a brilliant mind. It need not be a scholarly mind; it may or may not be a mind carefully organized at first-level details. It is a mind that can distinguish between important issues and momentary difficulties. It has very little to do with intelligence; it has to do with imagination and perception. Some teachers have an almost instinctive perception of the central issues involved in any given situation; other teachers must sit down to study all aspects before the central issues come into focus. Whatever may be the individual variations on the theme, the best music teachers have a rather clearly defined idea of the specific task of the moment and a clearly outlined vision of the final stage of the operation.

Third, the best music teachers have a capacity for sustained thrust. Many bright young music teachers show all evidence of promise, but they retreat in the face of scheduling problems, budget conflicts, interruptions in their instructional program, broken horns, misplaced music, discipline troubles, reluctant administrators, and lethargic boards of education. These promising young teachers often give up in despair and leave the profession. The serious professional, however, persists. He keeps his vision in mind, and he drives steadily toward that vision until he gets what he knows to be reasonable and proper for his work—full instrumentation for the band, or a string program in the grades, or robes for the choir, or a full array of substantial references in the school library, or a summer music camp, or whatever. The best music teachers have an extraordinary capacity for sustained, directed effort.

Fourth, the best music teachers somehow generate in their students a fierce desire to do well. This is a most illusive trait to identify. Some teachers get it through fear, some through love, some through subtle mixtures of each. But it is there in every good music teacher. Sooner or later the students come around to an intense pride in the music department and their involvement therewith.

These are, then, what seem to be the primary and secondary professional attributes of the best music teachers. If a new music teacher takes the cultivation of these attributes seriously, he stands a better-than-average chance for a purposeful and productive career.

CHAPTER 2

The Pupils

M any of the problems of music education in the secondary schools come into focus if the teacher thoroughly understands the nature of adolescence.

"The main business of the adolescent is to stop being one."[1] This statement may be the key to a better understanding of pupils of the junior and senior high school. Secondary school pupils are young adults in many respects, perhaps not yet fully matured, but nevertheless aware of the approach of adulthood. The adolescent is fully convinced that he is an adult even though he may realize that he is not yet in full command of adult powers. He likes to feel he is independent, free of authority, and permitted to make his own decisions and work for his own benefit. Although he is in need of the security of established rules and patterns of conduct, he is prone to resent and rebel against what he considers interference in his personal affairs.

ADOLESCENT DEVELOPMENT

Four aspects of adolescent development must be considered: physical maturity, intellectual sophistication, emotional stability, and social

---

[1]Luella Cole, *Psychology of Adolescence*, 5th ed. New York: Holt, Rinehart and Winston, Inc., 1959, p. 9.

adjustment. In each of these areas of human behavior, adolescents vacillate from angelic to devilish extremes.

In physical development the adolescent undergoes rapid and radical changes. There is a material increase in height and weight immediately prior to pubescence. A source of embarrassment to the adolescent is that his arms and legs seem to grow faster than his torso, making him appear clumsy and causing his clothes to become too small while they are still new. He will seem poorly coordinated, prone to tripping over furniture, unable to master simple dance steps, and completely inept in physical games and sports. He may seem to be chronically fatigued, always lethargic, and with a pronounced distaste for active games.

Paradoxically, the adolescent also shows gains in bodily agility and muscular control. He may be less agile and adept during the period in which his extremities grow most rapidly, but thereafter his development progresses even more swiftly. He may give the impression of having limitless sources of energy. His coordination improves, he begins to move with ease and grace, and he develops interest in activities that display physical prowess.

The adolescent often becomes deeply concerned about his own appearance. Because of obvious changes in bodily proportions among boys and girls, and the appearance of facial hair and the changing voice among boys, the adolescent cannot ignore the physical changes taking place in his own body. The adolescent may take pride in this evidence of approaching adulthood, or he may be ashamed of the unfamiliar aspects of his developing physical nature. In either case the changes arouse his curiosity about both his own and the opposite sex.

Intellectually, adolescence is a stage in which the pupil is especially susceptible to education. The adolescent is intensely curious and eager to find causes for both natural phenomena and social conditions; he wants to know why things happen. At this age, among boys especially, there may be a strong interest in science leading to experiments in chemistry, the construction of electronic equipment, or expert knowledge of internal combustion engines. On the other hand, the adolescent may be impatient with school subjects or with teaching methods that do not seem logical or practical. He will have little interest in memorization, preferring to learn through understanding, and will be impatient with the drill needed to learn unrelated facts. Adolescent interests are strong and varied. Once interest is aroused in a subject, the adolescent sometimes follows it with more determination and singleness of purpose than is mustered by an adult. If he encounters difficulty in school subjects, it may be because he has so many and such varied interests that there are too many claims on his time and energy.

Adolescents enjoy work that demands quick thinking and cleverness. Such work may be of great interest to pupils even though it seems to have no immediate or practical application, because it provides exercise for the mind and the developing powers of abstract thinking. This new capacity for abstract thinking occurs at an earlier age and to a greater extent than is generally believed.[2] It is a change as profound and turbulent as the adolescent's physical maturation. It is a complex transition from concrete to abstract cognitive functioning, and it occurs in adolescents of modest and average intellectual ability as well as those of superior intellectual ability.

Equally significant changes occur in the adolescent's emotional nature with differences among individuals wide enough to make generalization extremely difficult. The adolescent is subject to moods vacillating between depression and elation in unpredictable patterns and without apparent cause. The emotions are highly volatile. They lack the stability imposed by adult experience and control and tend to be intense and disturbing. Fear, anxiety, and frustration are created by the adolescent's awareness of physical and other changes and by the realization that adulthood is soon to offer an entire new set of experiences. Joy, excitement, and pride are created by new freedoms and the awareness of hitherto unsuspected powers. The adolescent's emotions are closely related to what he thinks and experiences, and manifest themselves in observable physical reactions. Of importance to the teacher is the knowledge that such emotions demand expression and can create deep-seated personality deviations if repressed. The emotions are responsible for many of the patterns of adolescent behavior, including some that are objectionable in the classroom. They can be responsible also for stunning achievement if channeled in desirable directions.

Among the most important factors in adolescent behavior is the desire to be accepted by the crowd, gang, or clique. Many adolescent drives and fears are social in nature and arise from factors having to do with social status. The desire to conform to standards established by his peers stands out above almost every characteristic at this stage of the adolescent's development. He wants to be well liked, respected, and popular among others of his own age and status. He will follow the

---

[2] For a penetrating and forceful review of the research to date on adolescent intellectual capacity, see David P. Ausubel and Pearl Ausubel, "Cognitive Development in Adolescence," *Educational Programs: Adolescence*, being *Review of Educational Research*, XXXVI, No. 4 (October 1966), 403–13. Summarizing the latest and most rigorous research and reflection in the area, the Ausubels build a very strong case for moving away from activity-centered instruction toward instruction at the level of abstract cognitive functioning as early as age twelve or thereabout.

crowd in matters of dress, speech, and conduct. He may flout adult authority rather than deviate from the patterns established by his associates. He chooses friends on the basis of group standards rather than according to compatibility with his own tastes and interests, finding in this way a kind of support not provided by his adult associates. He may be especially sensitive to factors of social class, family wealth, and background, and he may adhere even more closely to ties that bind him to his own social group. Closely allied to this need for social support and approval is the adolescent's tendency to select and imitate a hero, often adopting the idols chosen by his group rather than selecting his own.

The adolescent is, then, a curious mixture of extremes. Each youngster is a distinct individual, does not fit readily into any generalized pattern, and requires individual attention and understanding from the teacher. He is inclined to be introspective, subject to fluctuations of mood and emotion, and finds it difficult to explain his inner feelings to others, adults in particular. Deprived of sympathy and understanding, he can become withdrawn and recalcitrant. Given appropriate attention and motivation, he can develop intense interests and display a large capacity for learning. Because of his unique makeup, the adolescent may be among the most difficult teaching problems in the public schools, but he is also the pupil who can respond wholeheartedly to effective teaching, providing deep satisfactions to the teacher interested in leading youth to new knowledge and insight.

PRINCIPLES OF LEARNING MUSIC

Over the years two great clusters of learning theories have emerged: association theories and field theories. Briefly, the associationists hold that (1) learning derives from environmental conditioning more than from genetic potential, (2) learning derives from an accretion of transactional parts more than from a grasp of structured wholes, (3) learning derives from an accumulation of past experiences more than from insight into present problems, and (4) learning derives from measurable stimulus-response patterns more than from abstract conceptual ideation. Field theorists hold to the latter half in each of these polarities.[3]

In the literature on learning, several items of common agreement appear: (1) a learner can attend only one thing at a time, (2) there is a moment of maximum readiness for any given learning experience, (3)

[3]Dated, but still the most comprehensive and discerning examination of the complexities of human learning is Ernest R. Hilgard, *Theories of Learning*, 2nd ed. New York: Appleton-Century-Crofts, Inc., 1956.

the most effective interest-generating technique is a form of "ego-involvement" in which the learner sees a fairly good chance of emerging from the confrontation with his ego intact, (4) learning is a dynamic and fluid process, not a static and crystallized achievement, (5) spaced exposure to a learning task is more efficient than prolonged exposure, and (6) an awareness of a final goal or grand scheme gives the learner a higher tolerance for frustration and a greater capacity for sustained application. A word or two on each of these items will benefit.

A learner can attend only one thing at a time. The clarinetists in a junior band will find it difficult to satisfy this teacher:

> Sit up, please, and breathe into the diaphragm. Release the air with a precise action of the tongue. And let us be sure to keep our left thumbs at two o'clock. Blow through the horn, not into it. Let me see, now. Oh, yes. Keep your right hand down for that "g" in measure two, and watch that dotted-half in the same measure. People, you must be more careful about your dynamics. You were way too loud last time. Oh, be sure to taper off in measure four so we can hear the bass line. While I'm at it, chins flat, please, and keep the right index finger away from those side keys. Did you all tune up? Oh, yes, be sure to be on time for our rehearsal next Tuesday noon. All right, now, here we go. Ready?

Beginning teachers, especially secondary school teachers of instrumental music who are fine performers themselves, often try to correct a multitude of errors at every pause in the rehearsal. To really get at one error, several dozen concomitant problems must sometimes be ignored until the learners fully understand and properly deliver the musical material under correction. In listening lessons in the general music class, also, beginning teachers frequently give the students an entire battery of items to listen for. All to the students' confusion and interest-fatigue. "One thing at a time" is excellent advice for beginning teachers.

That there is a moment of maximum readiness for any given learning experience is fully appreciated by nearly all music teachers. Too much so, perhaps. Music teachers sometimes fail to bring their students up to full potential because they hastily conclude that their students are not ready for vibrato, or for Bach, or for third position, or for double-tonguing, or for a listening lesson on absolute music, or whatever. Also, beginning teachers sometimes introduce something fairly sophisticated and, meeting with failure, put it away, never to get around to it again until the following school year. It is best to be constantly on the alert for signs of readiness, and to keep testing, informally, to ascertain when the golden moment has arrived.

The motivation-interest aspect of learning is fairly well handled by most secondary-school music teachers. Two suggestions: (1) Interest need not derive from outside the music; look for interest-generating items within the musical material. (2) Try to develop a little showmanship; adolescents are becoming more and more visually minded, and a few gimmicks will do wonders in breaking their resistance to the academic message to come.

Of great importance in motivation is the adolescent's ego and his need for security. He sees each learning task as an opportunity for failure or success. The teacher should neither delude him with many false and superficial successes nor intimidate him with repeated, spirit-crushing failures. For example, if a student comes to the front of the room to do something at the chalkboard, the teacher should make every effort to find reason for a positive remark: "That is very close, Bob. Fine. Who can help out, here? James, what else might we do?" Bob has just missed by a mile, incidentally. The fact that the teacher is still digging for the correct answer tells the whole room that the job is not yet done. No need to break the boy with, "No. That is not correct, Bob. Sit down, please."

Learning is a dynamic and fluid process, not a static and crystallized achievement. A teacher must teach many things over and over again before the material will take hold. A wise music teacher startled a methods class, one day, with this statement: "I had thirty-two students in the class, and I had to teach the major scale thirty-two times in thirty-two different ways to be sure that I touched each child."

Nearly all of systematic instruction follows the rule on spaced exposure to learning tasks. A student has five or six subjects in his high school program, and he touches base in each subject nearly every day. Otherwise he would study English on Mondays, chemistry on Tuesdays, and so on. Educational psychologists and curriculum specialists are experimenting with fewer and longer periods of exposure each week. The results of the experimentation are not yet completely known. By and large a beginning teacher will find himself working in a traditional scheme of things, so it will be of profit to plan accordingly.

Spaced exposure to a learning task within a given hour's rehearsal might be worth the effort. An exceptionally difficult and important four-measure modulatory passage could be checked at 10:17, again at 10:34, and again at 10:47 in a 10–11 a.m. rehearsal. The results would prove interesting. Students are unaccustomed to this seemingly disjointed technique, though, and the teacher will have to carry it off with businesslike and good-natured insistence.

An awareness of the final goal or grand scheme gives the learner a higher tolerance for frustration and a greater capacity for sustained application. This is the instructional value of contests, festivals, concerts, and examinations. It focuses the students' efforts on a specific and, to them, fully justified goal. Witness the enormous lethargy of a high school

choir after its spring concert. A teacher might try to schedule a recording
session or a concert for the elementary school near the very last days of
the school year to keep pupil interest at a high level to the end. Several
new, lighter compositions might be selected for this very last performance. The genuine instructional value will outweigh all the scheduling
complications and administrative pains.

Human learning is a truly puzzling phenomenon. It is a little like
friendship—easier to describe than to define, easier to observe than to
explain, easier to preclude than to precipitate.

PREVENTATIVE AND CORRECTIVE DISCIPLINE

The best music teachers have control of the teaching-learning situation
at all times. Whatever may be the virtues of student-centered discussions, plans, and activities, it is the teacher who must answer to society
for the success or failure of the class. Strangely enough, the students
also are inclined to give their teacher all credit or discredit for the success or failure of the class.

Students' judgments go something like this:

"I think he is nice, but we are not learning anything."
"What a farce. He lets us do anything we want in there."
"He is all right, but last year we learned more from Mr. Jackson."
"He is really great. Boy, there is no nonsense when he comes into the
room."
"He is really cool. He even danced a minuet in class one day."
"Old Smitty cannot sing, but he is a great choir director."

The theme is usually the teacher, seldom the subject. Adolescents are,
after all, in no position to judge the value of chemistry, or Bach, or
American history. They are, though, in an ideal position to judge the
sincerity, competence, and effectiveness of the person trying to sell them
chemistry, or Bach, or American history. To be sure, their judgment is
based on an immature and incomplete grasp of the entire state of affairs,
but their judgment is, nonetheless, a crucial factor in the overall tone of
the classroom.

The overall tone of the classroom should be businesslike and friendly
but firm. The avowed purpose of the association is to learn something
about music, and the teacher is expected to control the exchange of information and the development of the skills. For all their complaints
about rigid rules and strict teachers, adolescents need and really want
well-defined boundaries within which they may test their unfolding
powers of intellectual and social behavior.

At the risk of oversimplification, the following guidelines are submitted for the beginning secondary school music teacher. Two areas of classroom control must be considered: (1) preventative discipline, and (2) corrective discipline.

First, to prevent misbehavior and all its attendant instructional problems, a beginning teacher should go into his new assignment with vigorous and obvious actions to indicate that he is to be in charge. Be firm, completely organized, straightforward, and completely in command all the way. Start the period at the sounding of the bell; let the stragglers come into a classroom already at work. Have pencils ready for all who will have forgotten them, or will say that they have forgotten them. Have cards or paper for getting names, addresses, telephone numbers, ages, and all other information that might be needed in the future. Announce the rules of the game concerning gum-chewing, tardiness, and absence. Tell the students how their grade is to be determined in the class. Announce the dates of important rehearsals or concerts coming up. Set the stage for the task at hand—systematic instruction in music.

Second, a beginning teacher should keep the students busy at all times. Leave no time for imaginative minds to get little annoyances going. Keep the students writing, or singing, or working at a specific problem. Avoid elaborate explanations and listening lessons, data-gathering procedures of undue length, and involved administrative details until the class is in complete control.

Third, circulate among the students. Get into the back rows to be certain the bigger boys are not tying the cord of the window shade to a chair, or carving their initials in the writing surface of their seating area, or setting up an ingenious prank. During written classwork especially, the teacher should circulate into the midst of the class, offering a gentle word of encouragement here and a firm word of advice there. The larger the class, the greater the need for knowing exactly what is going on throughout the entire room at all times.

Fourth, anticipate and eliminate potential trouble. The potential for greatest trouble is the seating arrangement. The more mischievous boys will always gather in the back rows. A new teacher will do well to get those boys up in the front rows where their behavior can be controlled. And separate the boys. Put a pretty little college-bound girl on each side of the more aggressive boys. The girls will be a little uneasy, but they are going to succeed in spite of all obstacles. The unruly boys are at such a loss for words and deeds by the very presence of the nice little ladies on each side of them that they often settle down into manageable gentlemen.

A new teacher should also try to identify the ringleader of the troublesome crowd. If at all possible, give him a title and job—Class Manager, or Room Captain, to be responsible for putting the piano and bench in proper position each day, and arranging the teacher's music stand, and checking the number of chairs in each row. The technique may fall flat; or it may give the ringleader the very thing he needs most and does best, a position of authority over his crowd.

Fifth, a new teacher should make few rules, but hold fast to them. If the rule is that there will be no gum-chewing in class, be certain to observe the rule consistently each day. A firm remark, "John, dispose of your gum, please," will do the job well enough. No need to assign tedious busy-work as punishment. The point is to do away with the gum, not to make an elaborate game of the problem.

Sixth, a beginning teacher should learn to overlook minor disturbances which do not really interrupt the flow of instruction. This is an art that must be learned by each teacher for himself. Adolescents are simply incapable of total and consistent application at all times. Their minds and muscles and emotions are in such a state of turbulence that they sometimes say and do things they themselves are ashamed of a moment after the event. A mature teacher must learn to separate the harmless remarks and actions from the really serious behavioral deviations.

Corrective discipline is a far different matter. There are times when a youngster simply steps out of line, and, for the overall security of the classroom situation and for his own good, something must be done. Each case is a special condition. Generalities on correction and punishment are seldom sufficient. A few guidelines may be of interest, though.

First a teacher should praise in public, punish in private. If a student does something well, an appropriate remark, "Good," or "Well done, Mary," in front of the entire class, will bring to that child a sense of well-being that can hardly be duplicated elsewhere. The remarks must not be overly lavish, for the other students will be quick to interpret the remarks as undue favoritism. Should a student say or do something completely uncalled for, a teacher must neither let the event pass nor make too much of it. A firm statement, "William, see me after class, please," will usually bring things back to order. When William and the teacher meet after class, it should be in private, and it should be straightforward, impersonal, without malice: "William, your behavior is simply not acceptable. Your comments are not appreciated by me or by your classmates. If this kind of behavior continues, we will have to arrange a conference —you, and your parents, and the principal, and I—and we will find something else for you to do from 10 to 11 each morning." If need be, the teacher should go patiently and properly through channels to the highest administrative level in the community to have William removed from class. There is no virtue whatsoever in a music teacher's trying to teach with a really dangerous or completely unmanageable youngster causing constant trouble in the classroom.

Second, a teacher should correct the problem, not the child. William may suffer untold psychological problems because of a pitiable home life, or a cruel stepfather, or whatever. Indeed, there is sure to be some serious psychoemotional problem at the root of his misbehavior. This is beside the point. The music teacher has a greater responsibility to the majority of the class—to teach music. If the teacher and the school psychologist or guidance counselor can work out a program of private assistance for William, they should do so, of course. But the first concern is the integrity and stability of the classroom instructional program. William's rehabilitation is not to be neglected; it is simply to be kept in proper perspective.

Third, a music teacher should make every effort to leave the student's ego intact at the end of the confrontation. The teacher should neither say nor imply that William is deceitful, unlikable, dishonest, or unworthy in any way. Indeed, the teacher should make it perfectly clear that William is not such a bad young man at all. It is simply that his comments and actions get in the way of the teaching job at hand.

In short, a music teacher should keep the entire instructional program on a professional level at all times. He should not criticize a youngster's personality or dress or manners in front of the class. He should not bring attention to any one child as a negative example. He should not embarrass or belittle a youngster for whatever seemingly justifiable purpose. The youngsters are entitled to their own personal views and opinions and mannerisms which the music teacher should respect. The job is to teach music, not to impose upon the students a set of preconceived values.

PRIMARY AND SECONDARY VALUES OF INSTRUCTION IN MUSIC

Education as an institution exists, however, specifically for the purpose of bringing young people to an acceptance of and a respect for a set of preconceived values. The paradox is that these values can only be demonstrated, not taught. Citizenship, democracy, respect for others, integrity, and all the interlaced components of moral fiber will find their way into a youngster's character only as he sees demonstrable evidence of their significance in society as he knows it. Students need and want instruction, not propaganda. They are impatient with sermons and lectures on ethical propriety. Teach music. Really teach music, and the other values will take care of themselves.

There are most assuredly specific values of instruction in music. It is because of these values that music education as a profession grows in strength and status as the great American experiment in public education matures and solidifies.

The primary value of music education is that it opens the door to Western art music for the youngsters of the nation. Without systematic music education, the door to Western art music might remain forever closed, and the overpowering magnificence of the musical genius of the Western mentality, from Pythagoras to Persichetti, might forever remain a mystery to a majority of the American people. To allow this door to remain closed to the youngsters of the most affluent and sophisticated culture of all time would indeed be a most regrettable condition.

The secondary values of music education are of somewhat lesser philosophical significance, but of greater and more immediate sociological significance. Music education provides experiences that are unique and difficult to duplicate in other subject areas.

Music activities, especially the elective classes and performing organizations, provide opportunities for membership in distinctive groups attractive for the same reasons as the crowd, gang, or clique. They are both elective and selective, implying that their members possess certain unique qualifications or skills. They are worthy and respected, regularly presenting programs applauded by adults and other pupils alike. They furnish a firm basis for feelings of security, for recognition, and approbation of accomplishment. As social groups, they widen each pupil's circle of acquaintances, at the same time providing for the common interests and cooperative effort that help develop acquaintances into meaningful friendships. Membership in music groups cuts across boundaries of social class, wealth, and family background. Music talent is not restricted to any one social group. It is common to find that leadership patterns in music organizations are somewhat different from those of other school activities. The music organizations often serve as social levelers. They provide for a beneficial mixing of pupils who might otherwise remain aloof. They weaken the influence of cliques and gangs. They provide opportunity for boys and girls to work together toward common ends. Instrumental music, in particular, places boys and girls side by side, de-emphasizing the natural and growing differences between the sexes.

In performing organizations, perhaps for the first time, pupils can begin to see the need for group discipline. Although the performing group is completely dependent upon the skills of its members, so too is each member dependent upon the efforts of all the others. Each individual quickly realizes that his own work is inconsequential unless it meshes precisely with the work of others and that the only possibility for satisfying performance is in the subordination of personal desires to group goals. Out of this realization comes personal discipline and willingness to cooperate, growing from within each pupil rather than being enforced by the teacher. In few other school activities is there the possibility for building this kind of social responsibility and demonstrating it in such convincing ways.

Music is equally useful as a means of building self-confidence in adolescent pupils. Adolescents often make rapid progress when learning to play a music instrument, particularly if interest is aroused through membership in a band or orchestra during the early stages of instruction. The increase in skill coupled with utilization of the skill in ensemble playing is evidence that the pupil is achieving mastery, that he can do something well, and that he is worthy of the esteem of others. Through performance before audiences he develops poise and self-assurance that carry over into his social activities, overcoming the natural shyness engendered by the uncertainties of his age. Because his achievements are recognized by his peers and by adults, he develops a feeling of security nourished by pride in his accomplishments and the popularity he enjoys because of them. In performing groups he finds himself in positions of responsibility, accepting his share of work and credit. Through these experiences the adolescent moves closer to the stability and confidence he should feel as an adult, learning to control himself and his emotions, and developing an assurance that improves his social conduct.

In the area of physical development, music plays a less obvious but important role in aiding the adolescent gain control of his growing body. Studies show that certain types of physical activities can be sustained for longer periods when accompanied by music. The rhythmic flow of music tends to guide muscular activity into rhythmic patterns and to provide a basis for efficient timing. The adolescent, whose lengthening bones present new problems of leverage and whose growing muscles create new difficulties of control, appears clumsy and uncoordinated until he learns how to use these new physical powers. Boys develop bodily agility and muscular control rapidly in later adolescence, but they show little or no improvement, or even a decrease in agility and control, for a short period during early adolescence. Girls also show improvement in control and agility, making smoother progress than boys, but do not reach the boys' high degree of physical proficiency. For both boys and girls, music provides opportunity for folk dancing, conducting, and other forms of patterned bodily movement. These activities offer controlled physical exercise and practice in coordinated physical movement.

Instrumental music ministers to the smaller muscles and helps satisfy the adolescent's manipulative desire. Junior high school instrumentalists especially, and those of the senior high school to a lesser degree, show strong interest in the development of finger dexterity. Although they may be completely disinterested in questions of tone quality, phrasing, and expressiveness, they will often spend hours practicing technique, racing through scales and arpeggios with reckless abandon. This is the manipulative instinct which finds productive outlet in instrumental music, providing needed exercise for the smaller muscles and practice in coordinated finger movement.

Through vocal music the adolescent learns about the changing voice and develops facility in its use. Vocal and general music classes furnish opportunity to discuss the problem, and classes sometimes become deeply interested in following the progress of boys passing through voice change. The boys can be aided in many ways. They can be prepared for the approaching change before its symptoms appear and can work toward vocal flexibility and control through singing activities once the change begins.

The religious and spiritual interests of the adolescent are among the most difficult to express. Music is closely related to them, partly because it calls up subtle shades of feeling and emotion and conveys meanings too nebulous to be captured in speech. Music is an outlet for the spiritual striving of the adolescent and brings him closer to the spiritual world that interests and moves him. It furnishes a medium for expressing emotion and relieving emotional tension, providing the emotional catharsis believed necessary by ancient Greek philosophers for the health of the human mind and character. If emotional pressures can be reduced through vicarious musical expression, and if emotional stability can be fostered through controlled emotional exercise, music can perform a vital service in ministering to the intensely emotional nature of the adolescent. Music supplies a medium for expressing the ineffable, for saying things the adolescent is unable to put into words, and for expressing feelings he might otherwise be reluctant to expose to his friends or to adults.

Music satisfies the aesthetic need which is in everyone to some degree and which may be especially acute among adolescents. It satisfies the hunger for beauty in a subtle way. It can be interpreted by the individual to suit his tastes or mood, and can be enjoyed inwardly and privately without ostentation or embarrassment. Through choral singing, music offers a unique aesthetic experience not provided by any other art, the experience of reacting *en masse* to beauty while producing it with the most sensitive of all instruments. It is a highly moving and intensely personal form of creative expression which touches responsive chords in adolescent nature.

For the intellectual aspect of adolescent development, music is a subject which can and does stimulate intense interest. The theory and techniques of music supply ample material for the adolescent's interest in intellectual exercise and cleverness. Properly approached, such studies as harmony, music form, and acoustics are understandable to adolescents and serve to introduce them to a facet of music which is intellectually challenging and which serves to deepen understanding and appreciation. The rewards of music performance can be sufficiently attractive to overcome the adolescent's aversion for drill and memorization, and the creative aspect of music expression is an antidote for the tedium of drill.

Music serves individuality and thrives on individual differences. In music activities there can and should be room for every degree of talent. Vocal and instrumental groups need both leaders and followers, soloists and accompanists. Music classes offer something for those who like to sing, those who listen, those who are well coordinated, and those whose talents are mechanical rather than artistic. Music has been influential in redeeming the pupil who might otherwise have withdrawn from school due to academic or social difficulties, holding his interest and enabling him to achieve success, first in music and then in other areas. Finally, music activities can be used to counteract the lowering of morale and interest among the school population as a whole, making assembly programs and football games more colorful and enjoyable, presenting concerts and shows for the entire student body, and creating outlets for many pupils with talents for leadership.

Music is an integral part of the secondary school curriculum. It is possible to exaggerate its usefulness, of course, but it is equally easy to overlook the many useful ends it serves in the education of the adolescent. In one way or another, music plays a part in almost every aspect of adolescent development. It ministers to social, spiritual, physical, and intellectual needs. It opens avenues to self-confidence, emotional stability, and maturity of character. It can do all these things if it is taught with skill, with insight into the nature and needs of the pupil, and with due regard for the special conditions of adolescence.

The General Music Class

CHAPTER 3

The Development
of Music Skills

The term *general music* is used by music educators to designate a class—offered most often in the junior high school, occasionally in the senior high school—which is "general" in three aspects: (1) it ministers to the needs of any and all students, the general populace of the school, (2) it aspires to a general survey of the entire field of music, and (3) it embraces neither exclusive performance goals nor exclusive academic goals, but goals somewhere in between, goals of general musical and educational propriety. The "goals" fall into two large categories—the development of music skills, participation-centered activities discussed in this chapter, and the development of refined perception, a spectator-centered activity discussed in Chapter 4.

The teacher of a general music class should address himself to four areas of music skill: singing, reading music, playing music instruments, and composing and arranging music. To avoid many hours of frustration, the teacher should remind himself occasionally that the music skills are being developed not necessarily as specific ends in themselves, but as the most direct and enduring means of reaching a larger, more general end: the capacity for self-improvement in music. This is not to say that the music teacher should not drive to the highest reasonable proficiencies in the skills. He should. He should hold tenaciously to his goals, and should be satisfied with nothing less than the very best singing by the general music class. But he should not try to turn the general music class into a showcase performance ensemble any more than a high school coach tries to turn the nine o'clock physical education class into a baseball team.

Indeed, the music teacher should approach the development of music skills in the same manner as the physical education teacher approaches the development of sports skills in the required physical education classes. The physical education instructor teaches the fundamentals of basketball, football, golf, baseball, swimming, tennis, bowling, and the rest so that America's future salesmen, chemists, and factory workers have something solid to build upon as they travel their separate paths of life. Ten years after leaving the public schools, a chemist should have in his common education the capacity for self-improvement in golf, or tennis, or whatever strikes his participation-centered fancy. And he should have a solid frame of reference for full appreciation of basketball, baseball, or whatever strikes his spectator-centered fancy.

Likewise with music. The music teacher teaches the fundamentals of singing, reading music, and the rest so that ten years later a chemist has in his common education the capacity for self-improvement in playing the ukelele, or singing in his church choir, or whatever strikes his participation-centered fancy. And he should have a solid frame of reference for full appreciation of opera, symphony concerts, or whatever strikes his spectator-centered fancy.

The analogy will serve to make another point. The athletics coach tells the physical education classes the very same things about tennis as he tells the tennis team. The instruction is simply less complex and prolonged, and the expected level of achievement considerably lower. Likewise, the music teacher tells the general music classes the very same things about singing that he tells the select *a cappella* chamber ensemble. The instruction is simply less complex and prolonged, and the expected level of achievement considerably lower.

The analogy between athletics and music as fields of human behavior may seem a bit contrived, but several interesting parallels occur. Both demand muscular control, speed, coordination, endurance, training, and systematic instruction. Both require intellectual agility, near-instant decision-making facility, and fierce determination. Instructors in each field are expected by society to produce winning showcase performance groups and intelligent spectator-audiences. Brilliant performers may or may not be brilliant teachers. Financial returns at anything below the superstar category are none too high. The most highly developed professional groups, whether baseball teams or symphony orchestras, compete against mass entertainment media for live audiences.

Enough said. The analogy suffices to bring the instructional responsibility of the teacher of general music classes into bold relief. This responsibility is to develop certain music skills, discussed herewith, and to develop certain powers of refined perception, discussed in Chapter 4.

SINGING

The human voice is not only the most sensitive and personal of all music instruments; it is also the universal instrument, the one most natural and convenient to each member of the general music class. It is the means through which each pupil can achieve performing satisfaction and feel living contact with music. It is the one avenue along which almost every pupil could progress toward active membership in a performing group during adult life. The development of singing skill is properly an objective of the general music class, particularly since pupils in the class are either in or near the stage of voice change. If the general music class guides vocal development and supervises vocal practice during this crucial period, it preserves vocal ability and interest for later school years and adult life.

Voice Change Among Boys

Prior to voice change, boys sing with a quality often called "flute-like" in a range essentially that of the treble staff. The tone is light, pure, and clear, possessing tonal beauty which for centuries has given boys' voices places of prominence in church music. When adolescence arrives, the beauty and flexibility of the child's voice disappears. The voice sometimes becomes unmanageable without warning so that boys who sing well one day may be quite unable to sing the next. In general, however, the approach of voice change is gradual rather than abrupt, heralded by certain observable symptoms. The beginning of voice change appears at almost any grade from the sixth to the ninth, but it seems to affect a larger number of boys during the eighth grade than during any other.

Among the advance symptoms shown by boys is rapid increase in body size, a better index of approaching voice change than chronological age. Facial characteristics begin to change. The nose and lips begin their mutation from childlike roundness and softness to the distinctly chiseled features of the adult. Facial hair appears and the Adam's apple begins to be apparent. Signs of change are noted in the speaking voice. It loses its childish, piping quality and begins to grow heavier and thicker.

As the voice of the boy begins to change, the first symptom observable in the singing voice is often a thickening of quality. The voice will seem heavier and more difficult to manage, losing some of its easy flexibility. There may be some reduction in the compass of the voice also, the upper tones becoming strained and shrill or perhaps no longer attainable.

The next definable stage is what has been called "alto-tenor," a term invented to describe the changing voice of the boy during a period in which it retains the alto quality of the changing voice but approaches the range of the adult tenor. At this point the voice is usually lower in register and perhaps further reduced in compass. It often sounds husky and strained, as though the tone is being produced with great difficulty. It may "break," slipping from bass to treble without warning and causing great embarrassment to the boy. Some boys of this category are able to sing only within a very narrow compass, perhaps in the interval of a third or a fourth near or immediately below middle C. Other boys may have two distinctly separate voices, one of lower register approaching that of the adult male and one of higher register similar to the unchanged voice of the boy.

A third stage is often called "bass." This is a term used for the changed voice of the adolescent, despite the fact that the adolescent voice is far removed in quality and range from the bass voice of the fully matured male. The adolescent bass voice is often limited in compass, perhaps to an octave or less. It sounds husky and raucous and shows signs of strain when attempting to produce pitches near the upper limit of its compass. It is limited in flexibility, is hard to manage, and may continue to "break" in both singing and speaking.

Finally, the voice passes into a stage approaching mature development. It may drop further into the register of the male baritone or bass, or it may revert to tenor. It improves in quality, losing much of the huskiness of the changing voice, and is more settled and easier to control.

Although it is useful in understanding the boy's changing voice to describe these four stages, it must be remembered that each voice has its own characteristics and its own unique sequence of qualities during change. The process of change is one of mutation, rather than one of a series of well-defined steps. Some voices do seem to pass through these separate categories. Others change gradually and almost imperceptibly from unchanged treble to changed bass, rarely showing huskiness or strain, rarely breaking, and with little reduction of voice compass during the gradual descent in register. Given proper encouragement and training, boys can and will continue to sing during their voice change without strain, discomfort, or injury to the voice, and will reach vocal maturity without having lost the skill or the pleasure of singing.

Voice Change Among Girls

The unchanged voice of the girl, like that of the boy, lies more or less within the treble staff and is clear and sweet in quality. It changes during adolescence but without the obvious symptoms or the pronounced lowering of register of the voice of the boy. The noticeable difference between the voice of the girl and that of the woman is one of maturity. The mature voice has power and a richness of quality absent from the child voice, but in many instances shows only minor differences in register and compass. It is the absence of well-defined symptoms that makes it difficult to detect vocal problems among girls. The principal symptom is one of quality; the tone loses its purity and becomes husky or breathy. Some may sound strained or weak, the higher pitches sounding as though they are produced with effort, and there may be a pronounced preference for lower parts.

Many girls find the voice difficult to control at this stage, to such an extent that they sing out of tune even when pitches are within comfortable range. This is a matter that merits special attention. The problems experienced by the boy are so apparent that he is aware of his difficulty and either sings in tune, if he can, or remains silent. Girls tend to be less aware of their difficulties and to continue singing, apparently insensitive to matters of intonation. It may be partly for this reason that there seem to be more out-of-tune singers among girls than among boys during late adolescence.

In the general music class the problem of the changing voice demands the constant attention of the teacher. Adolescent voices are immature and unsettled, undergoing rapid and constant change. Despite their growth in size and strength, vocal mechanisms at this stage of development tire easily. The fatigue resulting from improper use of the voice can cause adolescent singers to develop faulty singing habits. To preclude the development of faulty singing habits, certain fundamentals must become part of the students' musical equipment.

Fundamentals of Good Singing

Three conditions must be achieved in correct singing: correct posture, correct production, and correct pronunciation. First, posture: (1) sit erect, six inches or more away from the back of the chair, feet somewhat underneath the body so that a standing position might be assumed at will, (2) lift the rib cage high, (3) relax and lower the shoulders, keeping the rib cage lifted high, and (4) breathe deep into the diaphragm, expanding at the waist. Easy to say. But most difficult to get adolescents to do each time they sing. Some kind of system must be developed that will bring the youngsters to this correct posture each time for serious singing. A chord at the piano, or a few simple statements, "Positions" (pause), "ready, sing," will do the job nicely. For the first few weeks of the class, the teacher will have to circulate among the rows of students, checking here and there, to ensure that all are really on the job.

Posture is so crucial to correct singing that nearly all else is unattainable without it. The youngsters must be so conditioned—and this is the precise term—that they assume the correct position by reflex action. They must be asked to assume the position each time without fail. Equally important, they must not be asked to assume and maintain the position at any other time, while the teacher makes comments or explanatory remarks, for example. Strangely enough, adolescents seem to like this kind of militaristic regimentation if the system is enforced consistently and purposefully.

If the students do not assume and maintain good posture when singing, no amount of rationalization on the teacher's part is acceptable. Beginning teachers often lament, "I have told them to sit up a hundred times. They just will not do it." Nonsense. Telling is not teaching. "I have told them to sit up a hundred times" is a forthright admission of failure. Tell them once, or twice, and insist that they do it the other ninety-eight or ninety-nine times.

Second, production: (1) conserve the air supply, using it as efficiently as possible, (2) open the mouth wide, but think of the sound as coming out through the front of the head, (3) vibrate the facial mask, and (4) spin a tight thread of sound out to the farthest corner of the room.

Third, pronunciation: (1) sing "on" the vowels at all times, that is, sustain vowel sounds only, keep the vowel colors pure through the greatest duration of any given note, and match vowel colors with the singers on all sides, and (2) execute the consonants with quick, precise actions of the tongue and lips, and exaggerate the consonants slightly to ensure their clarity and articulate delivery.

Singing is infinitely more complex than the above sweeping generalizations allow, to be sure, and to try to train adolescent voices in the fundamentals of correct singing in class-method circumstances is an ambitious, even presumptuous, undertaking. All factors considered, though, the above fundamental principles would seem to be reasonable initial concepts for instruction in singing in the context of the general music class. The music teacher who holds to their implementation with stubborn but good-tempered determination will be pleasantly surprised by the results of his work.

A word of caution. It is usually unwise to spend extended periods of time in general music classes in vocalises and elaborate warm-up routines. Exercises and drills, if necessary, arise naturally out of the song literature being studied. Other exercises not related to the songs under study are used as infrequently as possible and then only when their direct relationship to an existing vocal problem can be made apparent. This is particularly important when dealing with adolescents who want to know why things are done. When drill arises out of materials being studied, its purpose and application are apparent, but when unrelated drill is pursued as a matter of class routine pupils lose interest.

MUSIC READING

The question of music reading has been a source of debate among music educators for decades. There have been those who felt that developing reading ability ought to be the chief objective of the vocal program in the public schools. Others felt that the drills and exercises used to develop reading ability served chiefly to destroy interest and eliminated them in favor of a program devoted almost exclusively to the singing of songs. Still others decry the drudgery of reading drill but seek to achieve reading skill through other methods.

Those who would reduce emphasis upon music reading question its value for the pupils who enter general music classes, few of whom need or use the ability to read music in later life. Only a relatively small number participate in church choirs or community singing groups as adults, and even in such groups there are places for singers who do not read music with facility. Artistic music can sometimes be sensed, sung intuitively without the need for accurate translation of every detail of the music score, and that which cannot be sensed can be learned quickly through imitation and repetition. The need for accurate interpretation of music notation at first sight may be of less consequence than the need for large numbers of people who are interested in music and enjoy participation in singing. In the face of such arguments, some persons conclude that music reading is not of paramount importance in the general music class and that minimum time, if any, should be devoted to it.

It is also pertinent, however, to compare the value of the two seemingly opposed approaches to music interest, through participation and enjoyment or through knowledge and skill. Maximum interest and enjoyment come to those who possess knowledge. Music education cannot reach its goal of building for every pupil a foundation of lasting interest in music by refusing to teach its techniques. It is knowledge that opens the door to understanding, whether for the professional musician or the interested amateur; it is skill that makes participation possible and rewarding. Although interest, enjoyment, and participation are the principal objectives of the general music class, the extent of their development is limited by the absence of knowledge and skill. Music reading is such a skill, the important factor in music literacy, and a prerequisite to full participation in choral singing. If the interdependence of interest and knowledge is accepted, the problem becomes one of pursuing both objectives simultaneously so that each reinforces the other. The conclusion as it bears upon the general music class is that singing activities can be the source of improvement in music reading and that skill in music reading contributes to the improvement of singing activities.

Analyzing the Skill

Before attempting to teach music reading, the teacher analyzes the skill itself to formulate a plan of teaching. When reading, the singer first sees the symbol and recalls it as having meaning based on past experience; in rare instances, perhaps never, can the singer interpret a totally new symbol having no connection with previous experience. The singer then "images" the sound indicated by the symbol; he forms it in the mind by associating it wtih a tonal or rhythmic pattern in the repertoire of sounds familiar to him through singing or listening. Finally, the singer uses the voice to reproduce the pattern already clearly formed in the mind by associating it with a tonal or rhythmic pattern in the reper- and prompting its adjustment if necessary.

Thus the skill of reading requires knowledge of symbols, a repertoire of tonal and rhythmic patterns, tonal imagery or tone thinking, vocal ability to produce tones accurate in pitch and duration, and aural ability to discriminate between like and unlike tonal patterns. With this analysis, the teacher is ready to plan the activities that lead to skill in music reading, striving to develop each skill both separately and in conjunction with others. No area of music knowledge or skill exists in isolation; each depends upon and benefits from the others. The act of music reading does not in practice separate itself into a series of well-defined and independent steps; it is an almost instantaneous reaction in which all separate acts occur so quickly as to appear simultaneous.

Building a Reading Vocabulary

An early step in the development of reading ability is the establishment of a repertoire of tonal and rhythmic patterns similar to the vocabulary essential in literary reading. These patterns exist in all the music sung, heard, or discussed and can be added to the tonal vocabulary without intensive drill in unrelated study of scales, intervals, and rhythms. They must be pointed out and are retained more easily if their structure is understood and can be related to other knowledge. The sound of the patterns is learned and retained more effectively if the aural impression is reinforced with visual and physical sensations.

The teacher directs attention to patterns in the vocal literature being studied and explains the manner in which visual symbols reflect the characteristics of each tonal pattern. To develop physical understanding, the class sings each pattern, conducts or taps those that are rhythmic in nature, and devises a physical response to those characterized by pitch differences. Pupils can play pitch patterns at the keyboard or using simple instruments and can draw graphlike pictures of each pattern at the board or in the air by picturing the rise and fall of the melodic pattern with their hands. Singing the pattern, seeing its notation, and reproducing it through physical movement, the pupil gains a multiple impression deeper and more memorable than the relatively fleeting impression provided by singing alone. At the same time the pupil becomes acquainted with the symbol and attaches to it all the meaning of the aural and physical sensations. Both symbol and tonal pattern are impressed upon the memory in a manner that associates one with the other.

Through such procedures, adjusted as necessary to fit the age and ability of the pupils in the class, the teacher begins to build pupils' repertoire, establishing a foundation for music reading. This process is less systematic and less intense than one which teaches music reading through a graded series of drills and exercises, but it has merit in that it need not destroy pupil interest, is directly related to other general music activities, and can result in gradual but marked increase in reading skill.

First Steps in Reading

The first associations are made between sound and symbol when pupils hold and watch the music they perform. Although much of the literature sung in the general music class is learned by rote, pupils use songbooks, referring to them for the words of songs and becoming familiar with the appearance of notation even though they do not actually read it. Because the notation is at hand, it is convenient to encourage pupils to use it as an aid to memory while learning each new song or recalling the melodies of songs learned during previous lessons. The general appearance of the notation indicates the ascending or descending movement of the melody, its use of scale or interval patterns, and the recurrence of phrases.

By directing attention to specific portions of songs being sung, the teacher emphasizes the notation for tonal patterns already in the pupil's repertoire and expands the repertoire by noting new patterns as they occur. As a new song is learned, the patterns it contains are identified and imaged so the pupils may apply their knowledge to reading portions of the notation. As their repertoire grows, the pupils are encouraged to use more and more of these patterns, making a gradual transition from rote learning to reading. When the need arises, patterns are removed from the song context for discussion or analysis, for comparison with other patterns, or for use in drill related to the song being studied.

Drill is a natural outcome of the process. Its need is apparent when it becomes necessary to practice a difficult or unfamiliar tonal or rhythmic pattern, to review a series of related patterns, or to explore the differences among closely related patterns. It is probable that no melodic interval or rhythmic pattern is completely learned until it is isolated from the song in which it is first learned, can be produced in drill context, and produced again in the unfamiliar surroundings of one or more new songs. It is also probable that skill in music reading develops only through extended practice in a process that continues to confront the pupil with new material, encouraging him to apply his reading ability again and again, strengthening and expanding it as each new song is added to his experience.

To encourage the development of reading ability the teacher focuses attention on some aspect of notation during every lesson. Some teachers turn to the "mystery tune," notating a familiar melody on the board for every class and asking pupils to study it until they discover the name of the song. Other devices are of less interest, perhaps, but may be applied to songs being learned. Pupils can be taught to recognize phrases, at first because they coincide with units of thought in the texts of songs, later by being alert to the sound of the phrase and the symbols which indicate the pause of the cadence. This leads naturally to learning that phrases recur or are repeated, and to detecting recurrence through both the ear and the eye. Next, there is the repeated phrase which differs slightly from its counterpart, creating the question-and-answer effect of the antecedent and consequent. Finally, there is music form, a structure created from phrases, cadences, recurrence, and variation, all of which can be used to help the pupil hear and read music.

In a slightly more technical vein, pupils can learn about scales and chords through meeting them in the songs they study. Introduced in a song, the scale or chord becomes part of the pupil's singing experience. Removed from the song for analysis and discussion, it becomes meaningful and memorable as a music element which is understood. Met and recognized in the context of a new song, it becomes another familiar pattern in the reading repertoire.

In any or all of these ways, training in music reading can be made a part of every singing lesson. No class period and no song need pass by without making its contribution to reading skill. Music reading need never become drudgery; it can be simply another aspect of music, challenging, interesting, and valued for its contribution to the improvement of singing. Even the drill necessary to learning fundamentals can be interesting and enjoyable, as challenging as playground exercises in skill and dexterity.

The intensity with which reading skill is pursued is a matter of the teacher's discretion; the thoroughness with which reading skills are learned depends upon the teacher's planning and ingenuity. Music reading can be undertaken as a major project, the sequence of reading skills to be learned determining the selection of song materials, or music reading can be regarded as incidental to class singing, the skill developing more slowly as favorite songs each make their contribution to the reading repertoire. In either case, music-reading skill is derived from vocal literature sung in class. The learning necessary to the skill is meaningful in terms of song literature and can be applied immediately to familiar and new songs. The process itself can be enjoyable in that it is centered upon enjoyable singing and is flexible enough to follow the interests and desires of the class. Pursued in this manner, the development of reading skill is an appropriate goal of the general music class, leading to greater success and deeper satisfactions in singing.

PLAYING MUSIC INSTRUMENTS

Junior high school students are often reluctant to engage in playing the same kind of music instruments they played in elementary school. They want and are ready for more sophisticated instrumental experiences. Involvement with ukuleles, guitars, banjos, drums, harmonicas, the modern miniature pianos and organs, orchestral instruments, and the traditional piano will catch and hold their fancy more readily than will further work on recorders, autoharps, and the simple rhythm instruments.

A knowledge of orchestral instruments is a desirable part of the pupil's general information, permitting him to listen more intelligently to orchestral music. In the general music class it is appropriate to show the instruments, to demonstrate the manner in which each produces tone, and to discuss the principles and mechanisms that produce various pitches. Pupils are often interested in exploring the instruments for themselves, experimenting with whatever instruments can be made available. Some of the pupils may even construct instruments of their own invention and give a modest lecture-demonstration to the class on the instrument and the principles of its sound production. This kind of activity might well lead to an examination of the properties of sound, as such, and to all manner of stimulating discussions on the overtone series, on modern techniques of treating sound, on the latest electronic sound-generating devices, on reverberation as a component of current popular music as opposed to reverberation desiderata in Baroque organ music, and on related topics of interest to adolescent mentalities.

Members of the general music class who play music instruments should be encouraged to perform for their classmates, however outrageous the instruments and the music may be to the teacher's refined sensibilities. If the teacher can bring himself to tolerate a ten-minute rock 'n' roll recital in the general music class, hundreds of solid concepts might be laid down with interest at an all-time high. From any given rock 'n' roll recital, for example, several instructional doors might be opened. Chamber music, perhaps:

> Thank you, boys. Very well done. Take out your notebooks now, ladies and gentlemen. There are some very clever and subtle things which the boys did, and I want you to get these things into your class notes.

The general music class may or may not go along with this. It is a little unusual for a teacher to come down into their musical subculture. Their feeling will be ambivalent—pleasantly surprised that the teacher would admit their music even exists, on the one hand, and mildly disappointed to think the teacher is going to try to enter and join their private and exclusive subculture, on the other hand. Whatever the reaction, the teacher proceeds with friendly but firm insistence.

> What you have just heard is what professional musicians might call a "chamber ensemble." This means that each member of the musical group carries the sole responsibility for a specific musical job. One person on each "part," or on each functional task. This is not always exactly true, but it will get us started in our examination of chamber music.

Did you notice that Bobbie's job was to keep the chords going all the time? And John stayed on the melody most of the time? Correct me if I am wrong, boys, but I believe that John plays what is known as "lead guitar," and Bobbie plays what is known as "rhythm guitar."

John's title is fairly accurate; he plays melody most of the time. Bobbie's title is not precise, though, for he does more than play just rhythm; he plays the basic pattern of chords in rhythmic regularity.

As sometimes happens in chamber music, Bobbie's job is a single job, but the result is a twofold contribution to the musical presentation.

What is Bill's primary task?

Bill has never before in his life been so involved in the general music class. He has an enormous ego-investment in this discussion. There is a good chance he is looking at the floor at this moment.

Yes, I know that he just sang. But what musical function did his singing have in the total production?

The class wants desperately to come up with the correct response, for Bill's sake. They sense that Bill may feel his contribution is less important because he does not play an instrument. Someone finally tries a response.

Yes, he sang the very same melody that John played. Good. This technique of doing the same thing in two different parts is known as "doubling." Jot that down in your notebooks, please. Could you understand the words at all times? I could not.

There is a good chance the class will say they did understand the words, because they really did: they know the tune. They might also say that they understood the words—for Bobbie's sake, because they feel, instinctively, that his contribution to the group is valid, and they resent the teacher's line of questioning. If the teacher pushes the discussion carefully, someone might point out that words are not always of chief importance. It depends on the kind of tune. This is precisely what the teacher was after.

Yes, I agree. Now we are getting somewhere. You are right. The words may or may not be especially important. If it is a slow, expressive tune, the words are likely to be quite important. If it is a fast, rhythmic tune, the words may be of secondary importance.

Bill is considerably more at ease. And the class feels successful in closing ranks behind him against the teacher's unwarranted inferences.

The point is, ladies and gentlemen. When Bill sings the same melody as John plays, he adds the sound of his voice to the sound of the guitar, and the total effect is a very special kind of sound that could not be achieved in any other way.

Musicians would say Bill's voice and John's melody on the guitar are of different "tone color," or, to use the term used throughout the world, of different *timbre*. Jot that term down, please. I shall write it on the chalkboard. Prounounce it with me, please, now.

So the combined sound of voice and guitar gives us a new and very exciting *timbre*. This is a very significant contribution to the total musical production.

Meanwhile, Charles, the pianist who plays that miniature, four-octave electronic wonder, and Joseph, the drummer, are getting a little curious to know what their function really is.

Did you notice, also, that Charles sometimes played the melody along with John, at the guitar, and with Bobbie's voice? There was a difference, though. Charles played the melody an octave higher than the other two. What do you suppose this technique is called?

Charles thinks he knows, and he feels compelled to try. After all, he played it.

"Octave doubling?" That is a good answer, Charles. Musicians might very well use those words. More frequently, perhaps, they would say, "Doubled at the octave." There is a term which covers this: *registration*. Jot that down, please. It means that a melody is doubled at one or more octaves.

Joseph is getting a little uneasy; he has not yet come into the spotlight. He is due.

These terms will appear on your next test, ladies and gentlemen, so get them into your vocabulary. Know what they mean and how to spell them. Then, later on, I can use the terms when we are looking at different kinds of chamber music.

Now, for Joseph. He plays the drums. He is busy nearly all the time. What is his job?

Joseph sits up a little and waits for the verdict. He knows his job, and is fairly confident the class knows it, too.

What is that, Mary? Yes. He keeps the rhythm going. Good. Just what is rhythm?

The students offer all manner and variety of definitions. The teacher acknowledges each with, "All right, so far. Can you be a little more specific?" The students keep trying—coming up with definitions for tempo, accent, and meter. Finally, the teacher pulls the threads together:

Rhythm is very difficult to define. Your definitions were not bad at all. You gave me various areas of rhythm. Let me try my hand at it. Jot this down, please. Rhythm is "everything pertaining to the temporal quality—that is, the durations—of musical sounds and silence."

We might say that music moves forward in time. It really does not, of course, but it does consume time. We "move," for example, from 10:27 to 10:33, by the clock, during a piece of music.

This is a rather vague idea, I know, but try to think of rhythm in this large sense, and it will help us as we hear other kinds of music.

The class may be a little bewildered by this jump into such an abstract definition. There is probably no great value in trying to get too far into rhythm in its full sense. Suffice merely to establish the idea that rhythm is much larger than they are accustomed to conceptualizing about it.

Several things contribute to the rhythm of music. In our group Joseph takes care of at least two of these things very directly: "meter" and "tempo." Jot these terms down, please. What is the difference between meter and tempo?

The class proceeds with different responses until the teacher pulls things together again with something like, "Tempo means speed." "Meter is the recurrence of groups of pulses." The teacher continues as the class dutifully notes the definitions.

These pulses may be stated quite directly, as Joseph states them when he plays his drums, or they may be just "felt" by the way the melodies and harmonies go about their business.

The teacher follows through, drawing together all the ideas that have thus far been presented.

Let us summarize, then, class. Our rock 'n' roll group plays chamber music which, by definition, is music in which each player has a specific job to do, often by himself, occasionally with another player . . .

And so on, laying down fundamental concepts and terms that will be needed in lessons to come. If the music teacher simply cannot bring himself to try this kind of a lesson with a rock 'n' roll group, he might try the very same approach with a small brass ensemble or a woodwind quintet from the high school band. Ask the members of the brass ensemble or the quintet to wear their band uniforms, incidentally, when they perform for the general music class.

The players of rock 'n' roll among the general school populace enjoy a position of such status and prestige in the adolescent subsociety that the teacher of general music might profitably call on them as individuals, without a group performance, as such. Everyone in the general music class knows, for example, that Charles plays the miniature electronic organ in the local rock 'n' roll group. If the general music class is working with cardboard keyboards, the teacher could find no better way to capture and sustain interest than to have Charles demonstrate on his instrument while semitones, scales, chords, and the rest are being explained. The students will stay right at the job, especially if one of them is asked, now and then, to come up front to try his skill on Charles' instrument.

It all comes down to this. If the general music teacher wants to develop instrumental skills in class, he can facilitate matters greatly if he draws on the talents of youngsters in and just above the sociomusical subculture of the class. The opinions of the young heroes on how to learn to play a given instrument carry infinitely more instructional weight than the teacher could ever hope to exert.

The students also need and want adult idols, though. If the music teacher is an accomplished performer himself he should not hesitate in the least to play a ten-minute recital for his students now and then. And he should stay in his field. If Beethoven piano sonatas are his specialty, he should play a dazzling section from one of those sonatas. He should not try to play a popular composition to appease the class. They might sense his insincerity, and he will have done them, and himself, a grave injustice. If he plays something really dear to him, the students will sense his great love for what he is playing, and they will be surprisingly courteous. Adolescents are inclined toward inordinate hero worship and toward forthright respect for competency. The teacher who performs really well, on whatever instrument in whatever idiom, will stand high in their esteem.

COMPOSING AND ARRANGING MUSIC

Junior high school pupils are amazingly inventive and imaginative. They love puns, jokes, tricks, and quick-thinking mental gymnastics. They pride themselves on their unfolding powers of intellectual perception. They are ready for instruction in composing and arranging music.

An initial assignment might be to rewrite the text of a simple folk tune, bringing the text up to date in its essential message and in its vocabulary. The next assignment might be to set the modern text to various contemporary styles within their frame of reference—the style of the marching band, or of rock 'n' roll, or of a Broadway show—still preserving the melody in its original configuration. Then write a new melody that would be more appropriate for each style, for the next assignment. The results of this assignment are sure to be the most disjointed, undisciplined collection of tunes on one central theme ever conceived by man.

Or the reverse approach might work. Take the text of one of the current rock 'n' roll tunes, and reconstruct the essential message in traditional, classic English prose. Next, set the altered text to several tradi-itional styles—Classic, Baroque, Romantic—still preserving the original rock 'n' roll melodic configuration. Then, write a new melody that would be more appropriate for the revised text in each of its various traditional stylistic settings. The pupils may be surprised to find that their cherished popular tune, both text and melody, derives its musical validity from the very same musical components as any other style of music.

In these preparatory activities, the music teacher will have to show the way, clarifying the students' vague gestures and bringing order to their unbridled musical suggestions. The youngsters will be able to han-dle the assignments on altering the texts, but the teacher will have to do nearly all of the early work in reshaping the musical components. How-ever uncomfortable the music teacher may be in his first attempt at this kind of instruction, student interest is likely to be at an all-time high.

These early assignments will consume four or five class meetings, perhaps, during which time the teacher must give a small but specific assignment due at each class meeting. The students will come with an assortment of purposely bizarre ideas just to keep things interesting. The teacher must be prepared to handle these ideas with some detachment and skill. There are sure to be many moments of riotous laughter.

To bring the whole instructional sequence into focus the teacher must have a final goal. This goal might be a final composition deriving from the collective recommendations of the entire class, or it might be a separate composition, however modest, by each individual class member. In either case the composition might be a new school song, an alma mater or fight song, for example, a traditional art song, an original popular ballad, a march for the band, or an athemlike selection for the choir. Something within their frame of reference is best. Something just a bit above their popular idiom is most desirable. The possibilities are un-limited.

The whole point is this. Nonmusicians of all ages are completely bewildered by musical composition. They suspect that if they should really apply themselves they might develop some modest facility at per-forming music, but the thought of actually composing a piece of music is nearly incomprehensible to them. To witness, and even take part in, the process of composition is a most exhilarating and revealing educa-tional experience. However troublesome the job may be for a music teacher, composing and arranging music in a general music class gets the students involved in the musical discipline in a manner that may yield unanticipated and generous instructional returns.

The music teacher should not abandon the idea if it seems to be unsuccessful the first year. He will get better and better at it. By the third time through the area he will have learned a good many techniques of inestimable utility to him and to his students. The final compositions, to be sure, are likely to be run-of-the-mill pieces which any creditable composer could turn out by the dozens. Be not unduly concerned. The instructional value lies in the breadth and depth of the experiential involvement, not in the towering beauty of the final art works.

To come into the home stretch, then, the development of skills in singing, in reading music, in playing music instruments, and in composing and arranging music falls logically and properly in the curriculum content of the general music class. The teacher of general music must plunge into the task with inventive energy, with firm control, and with a long-range goal crystallized in his mind. The responsibility is heavy: to provide systematic class-method instruction in these participation-centered music skills for the entire general populace of the school. The goal is ambitious: to so firmly fix the substance of these participation-centered skills in the musical equipment of the youngsters, to so demonstrably enlarge their capacity for self-improvement, that they can hardly revert to previous ways.

If he succeeds, the teacher of general music will have immeasurably enriched the musical life of America's salesmen, chemists, and factory workers who are, after all, the general participants in the general music of the land.

CHAPTER 4

The Development
of Refined Perception

Having considered the first major goal of the general music class—the development of certain participation-centered music skills: singing, reading music, playing music instruments, and composing and arranging music—it now remains to examine the second major goal, an enlargement of the student's capacity for self-improvement in what might be called a spectator-centered concern: the development of refined perception.

VALUE

The greatest problem in trying to develop refined powers of perception among adolescents is the music teacher's perfectly natural inclination to try to convince the youngsters that Beethoven is better than the Beatles. It cannot be done. Nor should it be tried. The teacher's job is to instruct, not to indoctrinate. He should set out to explain, to describe, to analyze, to point out, to examine, to draw attention to, to lead the students into discovering things in the music of Beethoven they might never have discovered had they not been enrolled in the general music class.

Beethoven is not, after all, "better" than the Beatles. He is different, completely different. He is more complex, more carefully controlled, more subtle, more involved, more refined, more difficult to penetrate, more

47

intellectual, more demanding, more sophisticated. But he is not "better." Beethoven worked with melodies, harmonies, rhythms, formal gestures, and came up with symphonies, each one a masterpiece, the very best of its kind. The Beatles work with the very same musical ingredients, and they have come up with several long-playing records, each one a "masterpiece," the very best of its kind. The raw materials of the two operations are identical, but the final results are completely, irreconcilably different. To assign value to the two different objects—a symphony as opposed to a collection of popular tunes—is to get ensnared in issues quite beyond the scope and sequence of the junior high school general music class.

Though composed of the same raw materials, certain phenomena which spring from completely different needs and which fulfill completely different functions cannot and should not be compared. Goethe's *Faust* is not "better" than Al Capp's *Li'l Abner*. A palace is not "better" than a bungalow. Picasso is not "better" than Walt Disney. A Greyhound Bus is not "better" than a Volkswagen. An ocean liner is not "better" than a canoe.

It is entirely possible, and for instructional purposes quite profitable, to point out that the ocean liner and the canoe succeed in staying afloat because they obey the same laws of physics. Likewise, that Goethe and Al Capp dig at their audience for the same human foibles. But it makes no sense at all to tell people to stop reading *Li'l Abner* because *Faust* is so much more sophisticated. In effect, music teachers come close to doing just this. They suggest, or at least intimate, that their students should stop listening to the Beatles because Beethoven is so much more sophisticated. Quite understandably, the students resist, resent, and ignore this line of reasoning.

TRAINING THE EAR

If the music teacher thinks of training the ear, rather than teaching the child, he will get off to a good start. As a hunter trains his son to hunt, so a music teacher should train his students to listen. To the hunter every broken twig, every slightest rustle in the bushes, all the sights and sounds and smells of the forest are exciting messages to be sifted and sorted and assembled as he works his way along, tracking the deer or the bear. To train his son he draws the boy's attention to a bit of evidence and, ten minutes later, reminds the boy of that evidence, for it suddenly takes on greater meaning, now, as they get closer and closer to their prey. The boy learns to be on the alert for certain kinds of details, to dismiss some and to hold others in his mind as he searches for new information, and to withhold judgment for extended periods of time until the exciting bits of evidence fall into place.

The music listener-in-training learns in the same manner. He consciously directs careful and sustained attention to the music, recognizes each pattern of sound, follows the tonal patterns as they succeed each other in time, retains in his memory what has passed, imagines what has not yet been heard, and exercises intellectual powers to interpret the pattern created by the succession of musical sounds. And to perceive, identify, understand, and remember the sounds of music, the pupil must have a repertoire of music knowledge from which to select labels for the sounds he hears. This is the area of music theory, but it is applied theory in that it is used by the pupil as he thinks about music.

THEORY

Music theory deals with music itself and with its nature. In the general music class especially, it should not be a series of exercises in intellectual discipline or in learning rules about music. Music theory is significant in the general music class only as it aids the listener, helping him enjoy, understand, and appreciate Western art music. It is meaningful only as it is applied, helping the listener to perceive tonal patterns and combinations, to understand them and to respond to them in an intelligent way. In planning work in the area of music theory, the teacher considers the needs of pupils, being guided by a knowledge of what the pupil needs immediately and what will be of use to him in the future.

This is not to imply that music theory in the general music class should avoid investigation of the technical aspects of music. The teacher accepts the fact that pupils are able to learn music theory and that they must learn in order to become intelligent, appreciative listeners. Musicianship requires knowledge, and feeling is more acute when it is based on understanding. A student learns to listen by hearing a great deal of music, by striving constantly to focus attention upon the music being heard, and by accumulating an ever-increasing store of knowledge about the nature and variety of musical sounds. It is the last of these that makes music intelligible; it is knowledge that directs the focus of attention and permits the listener to sustain perceptive attention while hearing large quantities of music.

It is not music theory that discourages pupil interest but the manner of teaching it. If it is taught in the general music class from the listener's point of view, and functionally applied to other areas of study, it is a source of exciting music discoveries. Music theory can derive from singing activities, listening activities, rhythmic activities, the study of music literature and history—from every phase of the work in general music.

Music theory has a twofold objective in that it is concerned both with the intellect and with feelings, striving to increase the pupil's sensitivities in both areas. Through the increase in these powers it builds discriminating tastes. It accepts the necessity for understanding the structure of music and the reasons for music's expressive effects. It increases the pupil's ability to analyze both aurally and visually, and tends to improve reading and performing skills. It adjusts its objectives and procedures to pupil needs and avoids any tendency to give undue emphasis to rules not immediately applicable to the listening experience.

Music theory is sometimes thought of as facts of key and meter, scale and chord structure, form and notation. But this is only a portion of the subject matter of music theory significant to the pupil in the general music class. Ear training is part of music theory and is closely related to the acquisition of knowledge about music structure. Solfège, the skill of reading music for the voice, is music theory and depends upon both knowledge and aural ability. Keyboard harmony and the ability to play "by ear" are applications of music theory and are properly included in its study. Laws of science are the foundation for many of the traditional rules of music and serve to explain its effects. Creative work is the application of theoretical knowledge. In short, almost every aspect of music has theoretical components and may rightly be included in the study of music theory.

Although the chief objective of instruction in music theory is a broad one related to music appreciation, the immediate goals of daily teaching have to do with specific knowledge and are selected to guide the planning of each lesson. Music theory requires the exercise of ear, eye, and mind, and it is the daily task of the teacher to develop these faculties both separately and together. Pupils gain new knowledge of some element of music from every class meeting—the feeling of two-four meter, the sound of a minor triad, the knowledge of a perfect fifth, the duration of a dotted quarter note, the effect of a plagal cadence, or some other concrete knowledge of music structure. In each lesson they learn the correct name of the element studied, learn to hear and feel it in music, and develop the ability to recognize and identify it immediately.

This knowledge is applied in each activity of the class, the attention of the pupils being directed to the structural elements of the music they meet while singing, listening, or playing instruments. They are also encouraged to apply their knowledge by referring to it in class discussion, using correct terminology, and in any reading they may do by recognizing and understanding the terms learned in class. The teacher helps pupils apply their knowledge in music reading, the knowledge gained through music theory aiding them in imaging sounds as they see notation. The teacher's goal is to plan each lesson to achieve all these ends, choosing a fact to be learned, choosing music for singing, listening, and playing in which it can be studied initially and observed in a variety of settings, devising class procedures that help pupils hear, feel, and understand it.

In planning lessons the teacher thinks of activities that foster learning. First, there is aural analysis. During both singing and listening, pupils are asked to listen for specific intervals, scale lines, rhythm patterns, chord colors, and so forth, responding in some suitable way when they recognize the item they are studying. The goal of listening may be to recognize elements as simple as the leap of an octave in a melodic line or as complex as a rondo form in symphonic music.

Second, there is visual analysis. Pupils are given every opportunity to read the symbols for tone and rhythm patterns they learn, analyzing and reading the new songs, following and singing excerpts from listening lessons notated on the board, and playing instruments. On rare occasions there may be opportunities for transposition when songs are beyond the range of voices in the class or in awkward keys for the instruments at hand.

Third, there is performing activity that permits the pupil to experience what he learns through direct, personal contact with music. The music that contains the element to be studied is performed through singing and the use of keyboard and other instruments. Excerpts from the listening lesson are sung, and excerpts from the song lesson are heard and played. Advanced pupils who do outside work in melody writing, harmonization, or composition have their work performed in class. The performing activity is especially important; it is the only way for pupils to experience what they learn in music theory, and it is the most productive application of their knowledge.

Other activities include writing original music, dictation, and outside assignments. These are not daily events in the general music class but are used by the teacher to serve a special purpose. Each activity is preceded, accompanied, or followed by suitable explanation, illustration, and discussion through which the teacher gives meaning and purpose to the activity.

The basic principle of music theory for pupils in general music is that it must be functional, directly related to other music work, and applied to every possible phase of class activity. Pupils sing and play chords and harmonic progressions, using them to accompany songs vocally and using the keyboard when possible. They apply the lessons learned about melodic structure, intervals, and scales in reading music and in understanding what they hear. They make similar use of knowledge concerning rhythm, music form, and every other aspect of music theory, referring to it constantly to develop the musicianship that refines perception and response.

UNIT PLANNING

The unit plan of teaching is especially desirable in the general music class in that it ties a series of lessons together. This is particularly important when scheduling arrangements permit general music classes to meet only once each week. Under such a schedule it is difficult to maintain the thread of continuity through a series of lessons. If the unit plan is used the central topic provides continuity for several weeks, a month, or even an entire term. Even if the unit plan encompasses a shorter span of time, the unit scheme and the manner of thinking it implies may be beneficial, improving the structure of single lessons and increasing their potential for stimulating interest and learning.

Subjects suitable for use as unit topics are numerous, but special consideration is merited by those likely to appeal to young listeners. "Music Instruments by Sight and Sound" is a topic of general interest to adolescent pupils. It permits members of the class to demonstrate instruments of their own and permits the teacher to bring instruments to class for demonstration and display. This procedure captures the attention of pupils who are intrigued by the instruments and the opportunity to examine them closely, to handle them, and even to experiment with playing some that are easier to manipulate. There are many possibilities for selecting music that illustrates the tone of each instrument and its characteristic passages, as well as for introducing such related subjects as the acoustical principles of music instruments, the related ranges and tone qualities of human voices, the music effects created by composers of different historical periods through various instrumental combinations, and the use of instruments to represent characters and portray moods in descriptive music.

A closely related topic is "Music and the Science of Sound." Adolescent pupils, boys in particular, tend to be interested in the mechanical and scientific aspects of the world about them. Here, too, are many opportunities for the teacher to generate interest in music and to extend interest in the scientific aspects of sound to the examination of many different facets of music. The acoustical properties of instruments is an obviously related subject, but the development of harmony and various styles of music composition are subjects equally appropriate.

In the popular vein, resourceful teachers build interesting units upon questions such as "Where Do Tunes Come from?" There are many examples of popular songs derived from classical music, of folk songs woven into major orchestral and choral works, and of worthy themes used again and again by composers of different historical periods. In addition there are examples of radio and television theme music derived from standard symphonic literature. In a unit of this type the opportunity to play tune detective may intrigue certain classes. In the course of the unit pupils can learn much about music literature. They compare the use of music materials by different composers, discuss the degree to which themes are appropriate to the words of popular songs and to the spirit of television shows for which they are used, and learn about the language of music through examining the changes in form, harmony, rhythm, and melodic pattern required when music is adapted for different uses.

"Popular Music Through the Ages" is a topic similarly useful to the teacher who wishes to begin with music pupils know and enjoy. Starting with popular songs of the day, it can progress to music from the current stage, music of the more enduring operettas, Viennese waltzes, selections from the operatic repertoire, dance music of the seventeenth and eighteenth centuries, and so on to limits determined only by teacher ingenuity and class interest. It leads to discussion of the factors that make music popular and memorable, the short life span of some popular music, and the characteristics of art music.

For classes with minimum background, a unit such as "Rhythm in Music" permits the teacher to utilize pupils' first and most natural music response. It leads to use of the exotic percussion instruments such as bongo drums, maracas, and claves. It can include music of almost any type, including popular and Latin American dance music, marches played by military band, the symphonies of Mozart, the vitally rhythmic works of Stravinsky, even choral music in markedly rhythmic style. It provides ample opportunity for physical response to music through rhythmic activity and can be used to motivate learning of music notation.

Equally rhythmic in its materials and activities would be a unit such as "Music for Dancing." This unit also could begin with popular music, progressing through folk dancing to dance music of other ages, to ballet music, and to the older dance forms included in orchestral suites. As rhythmic activity it could include folk dancing and the use of percussion instruments to provide dance rhythms. It leads to a survey of music history and the many dance forms found in orchestral music of each epoch as well as to discussion of the social and other environmental factors that influenced the development of the dance and its music. Both of these units, because they examine the rhythmic element that is close to the heart of music, and because they offer a wealth of materials to which pupils respond easily, can be of great service to the teacher in developing class interest.

"Pictures in Music" can include descriptive and programmatic music, surveying the entire range of music history. Opportunities for correlation exist not only between music and literature but between music and painting, sculpture, and architecture as well. There are, for example, interesting possibilities for comparing two paintings dissimilar in style with two music examples that exhibit the same stylistic differences. In all units of this type there is strong appeal to pupils' imaginative powers.

For more advanced classes, units dealing with music form, with themes, scales and intervals, or with harmony and its effect upon music style can be planned in a manner appropriate to the class level of knowledge and interest. Units including music of specific nations, regions, or peoples provide for close correlation with the work of social studies and other classes. Units can be adjusted to many levels of class ability, age, and grade, exploring the technical aspects of music or avoiding technical difficulties to concentrate on pupil interest and response. The class activities included in unit planning may be restricted to listening only or may be expanded to include singing, rhythmic activities, creative work, ear training, and playing instruments.

One difficulty is that the unit plan offers so many opportunities for engaging pupil interest through correlations and varied activities that the teacher may lose sight of the basic purpose of the unit. The unit that leads to constructing home-made instruments, drawing pictures, making costumes, presenting oral reports about foreign countries, and other such extramusical activities—and drastically reduces the time devoted to music to make them possible—becomes something other than a music unit and is not appropriate to the general music class.

WHAT TO TEACH

New music teachers are sometimes puzzled by the complexities of listening lessons. They are often at a loss for exactly what to teach about a given piece of music, and they sometimes wonder exactly how to get into a composition for the youngsters.

Beginning the Lesson

The critical period includes the few minutes during which the pupils enter the room, take their seats, and look to the teacher to begin the work of the lesson. If the teacher calls the roll, makes announcements, and distributes materials, pupils divert their attention to other things until the teacher is ready to call them back to the work a hand. If the teacher takes advantage of the first few minutes by doing something to arouse curiosity related to the work of the lesson, the lesson will begin and progress smoothly. For this reason the teacher gives careful thought to the possibilities for showing an object of interest, playing a unique music selection, asking a stimulating question, or in some other way challenging pupils as soon as they are in the room. This, too, is a teaching device and must be calculated in terms of pupil interests, unit topics, music materials, lesson goals, and other such factors.

For a lesson dealing with music instruments, a display of several instruments arranged on a table at the front of the room might be suitable. For a lesson dealing with the science of sound a similar display of equipment from the physics laboratory is indicated. If the lesson is about keyboard instruments the classroom piano might be turned to face the class with front panels removed to expose the strings and hammer mechanism, or the teacher might begin dismantling the piano, without comment, as soon as the class is in the room. For lessons devoted to descriptive or programmatic music a large picture placed on an easel or projected on a screen might capture the attention of the class, or the teacher might begin with a dramatic reading of the story or poem on which the music is based. For other lessons the teacher might simply write a provocative statement or question on the board, ask a stimulating question of the class, begin playing the piano or a recording without comment, or use unusual articles as "props" to arouse curiosity. In short, it is entirely proper and quite desirable that the teacher display showmanship in utilizing the dramatic potentials of music materials. Although it is improbable that the teacher will be able to devise a dramatic opening for every lesson, a procedure that arouses immediate curiosity provides an auspicious beginning.

Focusing Attention on Musical Ingredients

The teacher arouses interest in a particular music selection by presenting certain of its musical materials before the selection is heard in its entirety. Themes notated on the board and sung or examined by the class become familiar and are listened for as the music is heard, providing satisfaction as they are recognized. Other elements of the music such as rhythm patterns, harmonic progressions, forms, and orchestration characteristics are examined and discussed to stimulate curiosity about the music and make it seem familiar at first hearing.

Making the music seem familiar at first hearing is the key to a dynamic and productive listening lesson. The youngsters must have some vague notion of what to expect and what not to expect, and they should feel a quiet sense of achievement when things they expect to happen actually do happen in the music. They become, instantly, "insiders" to the musical event, not passive and detached "outsiders."

The preparatory or introductory remarks that are of greatest instructional authority, then, are those remarks which help the student get inside the music. Other remarks may be memorable and interesting but not pointedly functional from the standpoint of instruction. The fact that Beethoven was rude, or German, or deaf, or pock-marked, or whatever may be interesting and entertaining, but it is not really relevant to the music under examination. Peripheral coverage of anecdotal and human-interest information brings the youngsters not one step closer to an enlarged capacity for detecting a recapitulation when it comes around. And it is the thrill of detecting a recapitulation when it comes around which gives the youngsters a sense of having some control over things, of being insiders to the events unfolding before them.

In searching for the most relevant preparatory remarks for the youngsters, a new music teacher should ask himself, "What would I tell the boys and girls about the music if I did not know the name of the composer or the name of the composition?" It would still be the same thrilling aesthetic experience. It would still be worth their serious attention. It would still be a great piece of music.

By restricting his preparatory remarks to only those things which could be said if the title and composer were not known, the music teacher forces himself to grapple with the essential substance of the music itself. The music stands or falls, after all, on the intrinsic beauty and organic logic of its materials, not on the colorful personality of its composer or on the charming and imaginative character of its title.

Reteaching and Review

It is desirable that music heard in class be remembered, that the pupil recognize it on subsequent hearings, and that the survey of music literature provide residual knowledge of music of different styles and periods. Although general music classes often permit less time for listening than the teacher thinks necessary, there is time to provide for repeated hearings of works studied in class. Each additional hearing should be purposeful, though there is benefit to be derived from incidental hearings arranged for no purpose other than renewed acquaintance.

If listening experiences are used as a basis for music learning, one selection may be used in several lessons as a means of studying different elements of music, perhaps to show the difference between major and minor modes in one lesson and to illustrate metrical rhythm in another. Such purposeful hearings do much to create a lasting impression on the listener. Incidental hearings are useful also during the portions of music classes that might otherwise be wasted. In some instances it is possible to play recordings between classes as pupils are entering or leaving the room. In others, there are portions of the class during which complete silence is not required while pupils are writing, reading, or distributing materials and will not be disturbed by music played at reasonable volume. In some schools the public address system provides opportunities for playing worthwhile music during the lunch hour or before or after school. In still other instances, music heard in class serves to review or preview works performed by school or community groups or music presented on radio and television programs.

Each of these devices for providing multiple hearings is useful to the teacher in helping pupils remember the music they hear. Equally useful are the teaching devices that permit pupils to experience music in different ways, to perceive it through different senses, or to see different facets of its structure. The visual impressions created when pupils see excerpts notated on the board help them remember the music studied. The vocal experience of singing themes or harmonies, the muscular experience of responding to rhythms, and the intellectual experience of analyzing theme recurrence or other aspects of the music leave similarly lasting impressions. Each helps the pupil learn and remember.

Correlation

All music grows out of a cultural and social environment. It is influenced by political movements, social movements, and advances in scientific and other knowledge. If the music itself is not directly related to any stylistic, social, or political movement, the composer and his attitudes cannot help but be shaped by environmental influences that are then reflected in his music.

The teacher is aware of these relationships and in planning searches for opportunities to make them clear to pupils. In the general music class especially, this information does much to make music interesting and to give it living vitality even though it comes from what is in the pupil's point of view the dead past. The teacher seeks ways to show pupils the manner in which each music selection grew out of social needs or was shaped by them, was influenced by political events, was affected by manners, customs, and dress, or is similar in style and general character to the work of other creative artists of the same historical period.

A more common concept of correlation refers to the practice of relating music study to other subjects in the school curriculum through active cooperation with other teachers. Pertinent social and political influences may be discovered in the topics discussed in history classes. Relationships to literature may be identified through the work of English classes. Physics and mathematics classes may deal with subjects pertinent to the acoustics of music or the mathematical principles that govern the function of music instruments. Cooperation is possible with foreign language classes, physical education classes, and other curricular areas, each area of correlation offering its own advantages to the study of music.

Correlation presupposes the regular interchange of ideas between music teachers and teachers in other subject fields. Through either scheduled meetings or informal conversation the music teacher gathers information about the work of other classes and their plans for future scheduling of topics or work units. If the other teachers have had no previous opening for music in their work, the music teacher takes the initiative by volunteering to include related materials in the work of the general music class, furnishing any needed information about the music to the other teachers as background for their class discussions. Once the pattern of cooperation is established, the music teacher selects materials or schedules topics to coincide with related work in other classes. Teachers of other subjects reciprocate by providing time for discussion of the topics that apply to the work in music.

Ideally, cooperation that begins with the interchange of ideas among teachers develops into an all-embracing unit of work involving the participation of many members of the school staff. In such a program all classes center their work around a common theme selected and planned by a committee or jointly by all the teachers concerned. Each teacher plans class work on the topic and schedule selected by the planning committee. The work of all classes culminates in a major activity such as an exhibit, assembly program, or play presented for parents and the community at large. Although correlation is possible on this ambitious scale, it is improbable that the teacher of music will encounter it frequently because of limitations imposed by time and the necessity for covering required materials in classes of an academic nature.

On a smaller scale the teacher of general music enlists the cooperation of other teachers in arranging related work on specific topics during convenient and shorter periods. Sixteenth-century English music might be planned for the period during which another teacher is presenting a Shakespearean play, or the physics teachers might present the laws of vibrating strings at the same time the music teacher is presenting orchestral instruments. Even if there is no direct relationship between the music taught and the specific materials of the other class it is usually possible for the music teacher to select materials related in some general way to the work in another subject. This kind of correlation is practical and convenient, stimulating interest and effective learning in both classes without interrupting the work of either. In the event it is impossible for other teachers to take part in a correlated approach to subject matter, it is still possible and desirable for the teacher of general music to follow the principles of correlation in planning music work, utilizing the subject matter of history, geography, literature, and other subjects in class discussion when it aids music learning.

Although it is desirable to correlate the work in general music with the work of other school departments, there are negative factors to which the music teacher should be sensitive. It is essential that material presented in the general music class be of high caliber and that inferior music be rejected regardless of its pertinence to the work in other subjects. It is well for the music teacher to be wary of projects not musical in nature. A correlated program dealing with South America, for example, might prompt pupils to construct Latin American percussion instruments. This is a worthwhile activity and one likely to stimulate interest, but it is ill-advised if it converts general music classes into periods devoted to carpentry and painting. Finally, there is the factor of time. Correlation is a time-consuming process. It requires periods of discussion for the interchange of ideas, meetings devoted to the broader aspects of planning, and extra hours of planning for individual lessons. It requires portions of class time usually devoted to music instruction to be freed for presentation of related but nonmusical information. If the process of correlation introduces too many of these factors and permits them to grow beyond reasonable proportions it defeats its purpose. Regardless of the obvious benefits of the correlated approach, it is not desirable unless it improves the effectiveness of teaching and leads to increased musical growth.

HOW MUCH TO INCLUDE

Because of the vastness of the literature of music, the teacher's first problem is one of selection. Criteria for the selection of music depend upon the teacher's knowledge of pupil background and the extent to which community resources offer opportunities for becoming acquainted with music literature. If pupils have had neither training in music nor contact with it in their homes, and if there is a lack of music activity in the community, the teacher turns to the standard repertory of music that is generally well known and has popular appeal. If pupils have had either training or contact with music, the teacher omits certain of the more popular works, including others that arouse pupil curiosity because of newness or contrast to music that is familiar. The selection depends also upon the teacher's approach to listening activities. The approach might be through the pupils' natural interest in popular music, through rhythmic response to music, through the relationships between singing and listening activities in the class, or through other interests or activities, each of which requires the selection of music suitable for that approach.

Following Personal Preferences

In selecting music the teacher is wary of following pupil preferences, choosing music to serve the purposes of instruction rather than music having no other usefulness except to pamper the tastes of the pupils. Adolescents are quick to express their preferences, to show pleasure in what they like and to express their opinions of what they do not like. When the class responds favorably to one music selection, the teacher is inclined to go on with other music of the same type, following pupils in a search for pleasure rather than leading them to music knowledge and appreciation. It is essential to select music pupils can learn to enjoy, of course, but this music must provide opportunity for learning as well as for immediate listening pleasure.

Similarly, the teacher must be wary of following his own tastes. It is improbable that pupils with little knowledge or experience will be interested in music that appeals to the teacher's tastes, cultivated through years of study and guided by strong interests. In dealing with a subject as indefinable and personal in its appeal as music, it is inevitable that there should be differences of opinion concerning the types of music that might appeal to the tastes of the general music class. Moreover, it is probable that each general music class will show interests different from other classes. The teacher can therefore assume it will be necessary to explore the tastes of each class by experimenting with different types of music, being guided by a knowledge of the music that has immediate and popular appeal and beginning with selections that produce physical, emotional, or associative response.

Developing a Checklist

As a guide in the selection of music the teacher examines the various ways in which music is classified, developing a checklist of selections, including each of the possible categories, and ensuring that the list does not omit any type of music useful in stimulating class interest. As a beginning there are categories based on the history of music, media or performance, music style, large and small music forms, and levels of popularity and response. In terms of history and style there is music from the Renaissance, Baroque, Classic, Romantic, Modern, and other periods. There are categories containing descriptive, programmatic, dramatic, and nationalistic music as well as pure or absolute music not intended to represent anything beyond the total beauty of music itself. Under performing media there is music for voices and music for instruments, including literature for large ensembles, smaller ensembles, and solo performers, for orchestra, band, and keyboard instruments. The categories under form are numerous. In instrumental music there are the symphony, concerto, suite, quartet, sonata, theme with variations, tone poem, overture, ballet, and smaller dance forms. In vocal music there are the opera, oratorio, cantata, operetta, anthems, chorales, and others. Where appeal and response are concerned, the teacher might consider such categories as popular songs, folk songs and art songs, musical comedy, light opera, oratorio and opera, dance orchestra, military band, solo concerto, and concerted symphonic music.

By considering some such checklist of music types and styles, the teacher discovers opportunities for arousing class interest, being reminded of particular selections that have strong appeal. The checklist is a useful guide for the teacher in planning lessons that survey music literature in accordance with the objectives of the general music class. It would be virtually impossible and perhaps undesirable to include all the possible categories while surveying music literature, but it is proper to select from the categories music that indicates the wide range of music types and styles.

Vocal Music

In compiling a selected list of music for listening activities the teacher avoids undue concentration on any one type of music. Many listeners, especially those who purchase phonograph records, turn principally to instrumental music and neglect both the large choral works and shorter choral selections. Choral music is worthy for itself and for the special interest it holds for pupils because of the unique appeal of combined voices. Choral music lends itself readily to class activities in which pupils sing excerpts from music presented in listening periods, permitting closer contact with the music and aiding learning.

Art songs and other literature for solo voice should be included in the listening repertoire also. Because of their expressive nature they illustrate an aspect of music sometimes not clearly apparent in instrumental selections. The teacher may influence the quality of the singing of the class by providing models of tone quality worthy of imitation by the pupils. For the general music class such songs should be performed in English. There are obvious reasons for retaining the original language of art songs and operatic excerpts, of course, but the controversy concerning translations may well be reserved for works presented on the concert or operatic stage. When songs are presented to young listeners, it is important that the texts be intelligible so the listener may understand the literary meaning of the song and the manner in which the music describes and reinforces it.

PLANNING FOR VARIETY

A teacher should always try to visualize the sequence of activities and plan to adjust it as necessary to maintain class interest and achieve effective learning. In many lessons there will be singing, listening, rhythmic activity, discussion, and other types of class activity. These are interspersed so there is variety in the lesson, so periods of quiet listening are brief and relieved by active participation, and so the sequence of activities leads to the acquisition of knowledge. Many lessons include an opening activity, a series of varied activities to explore, experience, and define the music element being studied, and a culminating activity in which the new knowledge is applied or experienced. In some respects the lesson is similar to a concert program, the teacher presenting music to an audience of pupils and being sensitive to the sequence of events in the same way a conductor is sensitive to the sequence of works when planning a concert program. Similar factors of interest, enjoyment, and appreciation are involved. The teacher who regards a class as an audience to be captured is more successful than one who regards a class as a captive audience.

Principles of Planning

When planning lessons in this way it is well to keep five principles in mind:

1. The "approach" to each lesson should be a device to capture attention and arouse curiosity at the beginning of the lesson.
2. The lesson should provide many opportunities for pupil "participation" in the work of the class and in the music itself, permitting pupils to feel direct, personal contact with the music, and taking full advantage of the adolescent's natural interest in procedures of an active nature.

3. The lesson should be conceived in terms of class "activity" in which pupils learn about music by performing it, talking about it, or in some other way acquiring knowledge and understanding actively.

4. The lesson should include "variety" to maintain interest, to provide for limitations of pupil attention span, and to offer a number of different experiences leading to understanding of the music.

5. The teacher should consider the "tempo" of the lesson as it is related to the amount of time consumed by each activity, the speed with which pupils absorb ideas, and the efficiency with which the teacher utilizes allotted class time.

The teacher calculates pupil reaction to each class activity and each music selection. He visualizes the sequence of activities and the probable response of the pupils, foreseeing what is likely to occur and planning for each eventuality in such a way that the class is led to the desired response. To do so the teacher draws on every resource of knowledge and experience pertaining to pupils, their natures and interests, music and its characteristics, and the manner in which music affects the listener. This is the area of planning in which the teacher exercises judgment and creative imagination to predetermine the success and effectiveness of each lesson.

The Written Plan

As a record of the planning and as a guide for the teacher during the lesson, it is necessary to prepare written lesson plans. They may be in either detailed or skeleton form, depending upon whether the teacher has sufficient experience to present effective lessons with only a few terse notes as reference.

Many teachers would like to have time to write detailed lesson descriptions several pages in length, including observations concerning the effectiveness of the lesson as a whole and its various aspects and activities. A plan of this sort is too detailed to be practical for use in the classroom but provides a comprehensive record for reference. At the other extreme are the teachers who habitually begin class with nothing more than a few page numbers jotted on a small slip of paper. This is not a lesson plan; it is virtually useless for future reference and is an unsatisfactory teaching guide even for those with extensive teaching experience. Between these extremes is the lesson plan which occupies only a 3 x 5 inch card or a page of significant notes, but which guides the teacher during the class period and becomes a record for reference. Such a plan is needed, although it is not necessary that it be elaborate or detailed. It should be referred to by the teacher during the lesson as a "cue sheet" or reminder of the sequence of activities and as a source of needed information.

Timing

In writing the plan it is desirable to estimate the amount of time consumed by each activity, to note this estimate in the lesson plan, and to make every effort to adhere to estimated time allotments. Although the teacher's estimates are rarely precisely accurate, they are essential if planned material is to be covered in the fixed number of minutes allotted each music class. In addition, the practice of timing music selections and estimating the time required for class activities prevents the teacher from overtaxing pupil attention span. As a guide for reference during class, the teacher should estimate the times in a column at the edge of the lesson-plan page, referring to them and the clock periodically to adjust the tempo of the lesson so it may be brought to an unhurried conclusion at the end of the lesson period.

Flexibility

It is often necessary and wise to deviate from planned procedures. Class attitude at the beginning of the lesson may dictate a change of activity. Pupil questions and discussion may disclose areas of special interest the teacher can use to advantage. The speed with which pupils absorb material may prompt the teacher to omit planned portions of the lesson or to expand other portions when it is apparent that pupils have not achieved mastery of the material. The teacher must be prepared to nourish every spark of interest as soon as it appears and to follow the lead of class response. Sensitivity to class reaction plays a large part in successful teaching, and the rigid lesson plan that prevents the teacher from adjusting class work to pupil reaction prevents effective teaching. Nevertheless, carefully prepared lesson plans are essential to good teaching.

THREE STEPS TO WESTERN ART MUSIC

Folk music and popular music are easily and immediately consumed by all. Western art music demands a certain enlargement of the normal mental and aural faculties. Three steps are necessary for anything like really high-level appreciation of this unique phenomenon, Western art music.

First, the adolescent listener-in-training must learn to expand his whole sense of musical time. In even the most compact symphony, not everything is always compelling and significant. Transitional and connective musical material is of great significance to professional musicians, to be sure, but this subsidiary material is confusing to the uninitiated listener. He is often puzzled by what seems to him to be a lack of straightforward structural components and an inordinate offering of nonstructural material.

In the music he knows, popular music, nearly all components are delivered in the thirty to forty measures at the opening of the recording. However colorful the last two minutes of the recording might be, the musical material is likely to be some fairly discernible reworking of the opening material. The typical adolescent listener thinks the same conditions will occur in Western art music. He thinks that themes will come and go one after another as they do in popular music. He thinks, for ex-example, that the second theme in Mozart's *Symphony No. 40* occurs in measure 10. He will raise his hand there, if asked to signal the entrance of the second theme. He is rather surprised to learn that the second theme does not come around until measure 44. When he learns to expand his sense of time so that he thinks in clusters of eighty and ninety measures rather than in clusters of six and eight measures for thematic units, the adolescent listener-in-training has taken his first giant step toward refined perception of Western art music.

Can every adolescent in the land learn to expand his tolerance in the area of musical time? Will every adolescent, whatever his intelligence, emotional stability, and socioeconomic background be willing to wait forty measures until a second theme appears? If so, fine. If not, what circumstances preclude such willingness? This line of thinking gets involved in what psychologists and sociologists call "deferred gratification," and there is no reason to assume that an adolescent who is accustomed to instant gratification in nearly all other situations will suddenly endure deferred gratification in music simply because his teacher has pointed the way. There is need for some serious and rigorous research into socioeconomic gratification patterns and levels of music preference.

In any case, the first step toward Western art music is an expansion of the adolescent's whole sense of musical time.

Second is the acquisition of a working vocabulary of terms. This is not mere mechanical memory work. A reasonable command of the terminology of the musical discipline is needed to enable the adolescent to assemble and relate the higher-order concepts and principles encompassed by and made available within the music he hears. With a sufficient body of abstract ideas that are clear and stable (cadence, motive, transition, modulation, interlude, first theme, second theme, exposition, development, fugue, tonal answer, sonata, recapitulation, episode, and similar abstract concepts), the adolescent is equipped to manipulate relationships between and among the abstractions so as to draw generalizations about the music he hears, generalizations which will be considerably more enlightened than the common I-know-what-I-like kind of judgments.

As his higher-order concepts and relational propositions become less intuitive and more rational, the adolescent listener is prepared to cope with musical substance of greater depth and complexity. He is also able to handle more intense coverage of smaller topics—cadence procedures from Bach to Brahms, for example—as opposed to less intense coverage of larger topics—the Classic symphony, perhaps.

The third step to Western art music involves the "meaning" of the music. An adolescent feels no urge to look into his own music, popular music, for any other than the meaning which is readily ascertained. The melodies are short-winded, forcefully direct, and nicely self-contained. The texts are forthright remarks on universal and eternal sorrows and joys. Nothing hidden here; nearly all is fairly easily available.

In his initial confrontation with Western art music, though, the adolescent stands benumbed and intimidated. He has read and been told that this music is not like his music. This music is about much more profound and exalted concerns. Music teachers, writers of textbooks on the appreciation of music, and even professional musicians talk about Beethoven's music being a great testament of the human spirit. Everywhere he turns, in program notes, on record jackets, in standard reference sources, the adolescent listener-in-training reads that Beethoven's music is about Truth, Fate, The Brotherhood of Man, Eternal Joy, and related Olympian subjects. The youngster is, of course, a bit intimidated by the whole thing.

He is a bit confused as well, for he hears no such profound utterances. He may feel guilty, for he has been led to believe that he ought to hear these things. And he may feel immature, for his teacher and other adults seem to hear these things.

It would be far more interesting, but equally insignificant, should the youngster learn that Beethoven was egocentric, unscrupulous, possessive, narrow-minded, chronically unhappy, pock-marked, deaf, highhanded, rude, and all the rest: equally insignificant, for none of these characteristics has any bearing on the music. Or, at least, none of these characteristics has any instructional value in training a novice to listen with discriminating judgment.

What does Western art music mean? This is a most complex and difficult question, and the answer must come with qualifications and in sections. Igor Stravinsky says that music has no power to convey any meaning. Aaron Copland says that music has meaning, but the meaning cannot be stated in so many words at will. All of which leads back to the question.

In the first place, Western art music has meaning for only that small group of people in Occidental civilization, perhaps one-fourth of the world's population. Three-fourths of the people who inhabit the planet would probably find Beethoven's music completely meaningless.

In the second place, Western art music has meaning for only that small group within the Occidental culture which has had sufficient exposure to art music for its fundamental gestures to have become vaguely familiar. This precludes millions of people in deprived areas of the Occident, and millions in areas which are self-sustaining in socioeconomic matters but not in cultural endeavors.

In the third place, Western art music is in the midst of explosive developments to which even the most knowledgeable and liberal professional musicians cannot adjust. The works of Stockhausen and Cage are often completely meaningless to the most open-minded professional musicians.

Where does this put a junior high school youngster in his search for meaning? What should the teacher of general music say about the music of Stockhausen to aid the students in their listening? There are no answers, of course, to these questions, and there is no answer to the question of the meaning of music. Music does not mean anything. It simply is.

A tree means nothing. It simply is. It is a magnificent and mysterious combination of roots, a trunk, branches, and leaves, each of which is an entire world of cells and filaments of its own. Seen often enough, under various conditions, by the same viewer, the tree takes on meaning: strength, or repose, or some similar psychological state of being.

Likewise with music. It is a magnificent and mysterious combination of sounds and silences which eventually takes on something similar to meaning. To search for the meaning is to miss the magnificence of the combinations. The complexities of the discipline are quite sufficient to engage the time and attention of the general music class without the added burden of trying to extract some kind of ultimate meaning in Western art music.

In sum, the way to develop refined perception is not to make a desperate search for the meaning of music, but rather, to train the adolescent listener's ear to isolate and identify significant musical gestures, to enlarge his inventory of higher-order concepts with which he catalogs and relates the things he hears, to increase his tolerance for deferred musical gratification, and to do so with straightforward and carefully organized subject units of instructional material.

If he succeeds, the teacher of general music will have immeasurably enriched the musical life of America's salesmen, chemists, and factory workers. The whole objective is, after all, to expand their appreciation of the art, to equip them for more selective and sophisticated judgments about the general music of the land.

PART III

Performing Organizations

CHAPTER 5

Administrative Necessities

One aim of music education during the past several decades has been to achieve curricular status for the larger performing groups. To make this possible it is necessary that the group conform to certain of the standards established for curricular subjects, including requirements for pupil achievement, evaluation of pupil progress, and systematic study of organized subject matter. It is also necessary that music teachers demonstrate to administrators and the public that performing groups are worthy of curricular status, meeting these requirements and proving through performance and pupil development that their work is rightly a part of the total educational program. If this is done, performing groups can be scheduled during curricular time, reaping many benefits from their status as regular subjects. More important, by keeping such requirements in mind the teacher is reminded of the true function of the performing ensembles and of the necessity for directing the activities of these ensembles toward justifiable educational ends.

SCHEDULING

If a given performing ensemble achieves curricular status, the group can meet regularly with minimum conflict with other subjects and extracurricular activities. Participating pupils are available for every rehearsal;

71

they are not forced to be absent by required school subjects or required to give up hours before and after school. Curricular status often permits more frequent rehearsals than a scheduling arrangement that permits the group to meet only during club or activity periods. It provides for the award of credit, permitting the pupil to allocate school time to music without sacrificing progress toward graduation.

The goal toward which a director of a large ensemble should strive is nothing less than regularly scheduled daily rehearsals during normal school hours. Daily rehearsals are especially desirable in the high school due to the natural tendency to expect higher levels of achievement from high school groups. They are also more practical and easier to achieve due to the greater freedom in electives permitted high school pupils and the growing tendency among administrators to approve credit status for high school performing groups.

The time and place of rehearsal is important also, affecting the success of each rehearsal and the progress of the group toward learning and performance goals. It is usually advisable to avoid the hours immediately following both breakfast and lunch. There is good reason to avoid the last hour of the school day also, and perhaps the hour immediately before lunch. At these times pupils tend to be fatigued and restless, not prepared for the intense concentration conducive to productive rehearsal. The ideal rehearsal time, then, is midmorning or midafternoon.

Despite the desirability of curricular status there are advantages in scheduling groups during extracurricular hours. Pupils who participate often feel there is something selective and special about the group that meets before or after school. They apply for membership and sacrifice free hours because they are interested in the work of the group and are willing to meet its requirements. Administrators are favorably impressed by the group that does not disrupt the school schedule by conflicting with basic subjects, but achieves its results during extracurricular hours by stimulating strong pupil interest. In some instances the only possibility for meeting a large number of pupils with a variety of responsibilities toward other school subjects and activities is to schedule rehearsals when no other school function is in progress. This applies not only to the hours immediately before and after school, but to evening and weekend rehearsals as well. If there are special occasions on which evening rehearsals are necessary, and if these occasions do not arise too frequently, the teacher may find that pupils accept such an extra rehearsal eagerly and that a great deal can be accomplished in one evening of intense work.

When there is a pressing need to prepare for performance, the teacher should arrange for sectional rehearsals. The sectional rehearsal is common among instrumental groups in which any one section may form a complete ensemble. But in choral groups, except perhaps those studying works for double chorus, a section withdrawn from the balance of the group loses its identity as part of the larger pattern and must practice uninteresting and unmusical material in drill-like fashion. Choral teachers, thus, are likely to have short sectional rehearsals within the normal full rehearsal, sending the tenors or altos to a separate room to work out a difficult passage. These little sectional rehearsals should consume no more than fifteen minutes, perhaps, for the students generally need the full choral components for maximum learning. Be sure to appoint a responsible section leader to handle the little subrehearsal; otherwise, the situation may turn into a conversation period. As a rule the music director should conduct all sectional rehearsals of the large instrumental groups himself to ensure consistent interpretation and full profit throughout.

ADMINISTRATIVE SUPPORT

Administrators are especially sensitive to evidence of careful planning and efficient organization. They respond favorably to proposals that have been considered carefully and in which every problem of organization has been examined. The teacher who wishes to suggest a change in the existing pattern of ensemble activities or the establishment of a new ensemble group is well advised to plan the presentation of his recommendation in such a way that the details of the proposal are clear to the administrator and so the proposal itself makes an immediate impression of careful organization. It is desirable to put such proposals in writing. The written description is beneficial to the teacher; it requires ideas to be put in logical order, encourages attention to detail, and clarifies problems of organization. It is also appreciated by the administrator who can retain the written proposal for careful examination at a convenient time.

Requests for school time, funds, and equipment should be specific, complete in all details, and considerate of the problems that must be faced by the administrator in approving them. Reasons for the proposed change are stated briefly but clearly. Inadequacies of existing arrangements are pointed out, but with good judgment concerning the work of other teachers and established school practices. Administrators are also sensitive to the educational benefits of school activities, constantly evaluating the school program to determine whether it produces results commensurate with the function of the school and with the broader implications of educational philosophy. It is appropriate that the ensemble director refer to the aims of education and the function of music as a part of the educational program. If there is any tendency for the administrator to regard music teachers as somewhat impractical, immersed in their art, and given to inspirational thinking, it is especially important that proposals emphasize music's contributions to educational aims and the specific ways in which the proposed change will benefit both pupils and the school as a whole.

Administrative support for performing activities also depends upon past successes. The teacher who can point to existing organizations with a history of successful performance and worthwhile educational achievement, and who is known to the administrator as one who does effective work, plans carefully, and organizes efficiently, is given the administrator's close attention when a new organization is proposed. Success may be the most potent evidence the teacher can offer. The administrator is reluctant to approve requests supported by the most lucid planning if he feels the teacher may fail to carry out new plans satisfactorily. The teacher must work diligently to improve existing organizations before requesting new ones, to make the most of every opportunity for music achievement within the existing framework of the program, and to propose changes infrequently and only when there is no suitable alternative. The teacher who appears in the principal's office regularly with plans for sweeping changes in the entire music program is given a cooler reception at each successive request. The teacher who first works conscientiously with the materials at hand and then goes to the principal with a carefully conceived plan for making gradual changes to improve the program is more likely to be given administrative support.

RECRUITING: CHORAL GROUPS

Talented vocalists can be identified in a number of ways. The cumulative records maintained by the central office of the school may include results of aptitude tests and notes concerning membership in previous vocal or instrumental ensembles. These may be of value even if the information is several years old. The pupil who showed music aptitude and interest in earlier grades, or who performed with instrumental or vocal groups, may be a potential leader in choral groups of the senior high school even though he has not been active in the music program for several years.

Additional information can be secured from the teachers who know the pupil through general music or other music classes in lower grades. The instrumental teacher in particular may be able to offer useful suggestions concerning pupils who have shown music aptitude and interest. Classroom teachers may be able to make suggestions concerning pupils who might develop into strong members of a choral group. The classroom teacher's more detailed knowledge of the pupil includes information not available through any other source. By making maximum use of all these resources the choral teacher identifies the pupils who would be most desirable as members of the singing group, discovering those with singing ability, musicianship, and interest.

Using Publicity Devices

Further steps in recruiting are largely a matter of suitable publicity and good public relations. The teacher grasps every opportunity to attract the interest of the student body. A bulletin board in the hall adjacent to the choral rehearsal room attracts the attention of pupils who pass it regularly. It can be used to display an attractive photograph of the choral group in robes or other costume, announcements of approaching choral activities, press clippings, cartoons, and posters pertaining to the choral program. Glass cases in the hall, often reserved for athletic trophies, can feature displays of photographs, choir robes, or other objects related to choral activities. The school paper may be used for feature articles concerning the choral program or a regular column devoted to the activities of the glee club and its members. Further publicity of this sort may be available through community newspapers, homeroom bulletin boards, and other media. Through each means the student body is reminded constantly of the existence of choral activities and invited to participate in an active and desirable program.

Recruiting Through Concerts

To further attract new members the choral teacher presents performing groups in concerts designed to appeal strongly to the student body. The choral teacher selects music for in-school concert programs to appeal to the majority of pupils in the audience. The music is rehearsed and polished carefully so that the performance will be as nearly flawless as possible. The choral group is presented in robes or other uniform costume to appeal to the adolescent's natural interest in distinctive dress. The concert itself is presented with as much showmanship as possible within the limits of good taste. This sustains audience interest and helps the school program compare favorably with television and other performances. A particularly potent stimulus is the annual concert, variety show, or Broadway musical. Similarly, the choral teacher may arouse general interest in choral activities by arranging for the appearance of outside performing groups in school programs—professional singers, community groups, or choral organizations from neighboring schools. By presenting choral groups in this favorable light and by reminding the student body constantly of available choral activities the teacher indicates that participation in the choral program is an exciting and enjoyable experience, a compelling reason for adolescents to seek membership.

Direct Recruiting

The active recruiting program is a productive means of securing new members. The usual posters, homeroom announcements, and newspaper articles announce the possibility of membership and provide opportunity to describe its most attractive benefits. Further recruiting can be done by members themselves, each being invited to bring a friend. The assistance of other teachers can be solicited in identifying potential individual members or in discusing the topic briefly in homeroom or class meetings. The choral teacher himself can do much to recruit new members, either by talking with desirable candidates or by being generally active in school affairs other than those devoted to music. In all these ways the teacher tries to assure the constant flow of new members without which any choral program must decline in membership and quality. As the program develops and more and more interested pupils apply for membership, choral activities can be diversified through the establishment of additional groups, and one or more of the organizations can become increasingly selective to raise the level of performance, each such improvement increasing the probability of success for the total choral program.

Enlisting Community Support

The support of parents and other adult members of the community is highly desirable. Parents are impressed by results. Performance, again, is a means of demonstrating results. Parents can be invited to attend school concerts. The choral group can perform for the Parent-Teacher Association, for churches, for service clubs, and for other civic groups. The teacher can address the Parent-Teacher Association, discussing the values of the choral program in terms of benefits to the pupils, problems that have been overcome, recent progress or performances, and the needs peculiar to the performing group. Demonstrations will serve to stimulate parental interest, the teacher using the performing group or selected pupils to show rehearsal procedures, techniques for improving the singing of the group, or for studying choral literature. This is appropriate for the PTA concert and might even be included in a public concert to increase audience interest and develop public understanding of the activities of the choral group. To sustain parental interest the teacher can turn to community newspapers, mimeographed bulletins such as a regularly issued "Choral News," and placards and posters announcing concerts and other special events.

Letters and Bulletins

Of special merit is the bulletin to parents that keeps them informed of the activities of their children and the requirements imposed by membership in the choral organization. Parents are justified in asking about school activities in which their children participate and the reasons for special requirements and extra demands upon their time. This information should go to the pupil's home as a matter of routine and on a regular basis. Parents should receive it in accurate and detailed form from the teacher through an official channel rather than in incomplete or erroneous versions relayed orally by pupils. The director of any performing group accepts the responsibility of providing either a letter to parents or a regular bulletin in which selected issues contain informative articles. In some instances when the student must secure parental permission for trips or when he must pay dues, a special letter is provided for signature by the parent and returned to the teacher. In other instances it may be desirable to provide a form to be signed by both student and parent, the form containing statements concerning the responsibilities of choral members and signifying the pupil's willingness to comply with the established requirements. In general, parents might be interested in knowing requirements for admission and membership, regulations concerning participation, dress and attendance, and the planned schedule of performances, particularly as it requires pupil attendance during other than normal school hours.

In some schools parental interest can be developed through the establishment of a "Parents Association." Such an organization can be of great assistance to the choral teacher and of value in the development of the choral program. Many activities can be discussed, arranged, organized, and cleared with the assistance of interested parents. The association can help in raising funds when necessary, purchasing robes and other equipment, and in managing and supervising trips or other out-of-school appearances. An annual banquet for the association, attended by parents, pupils, and teachers and complete with the presentation of awards to outstanding pupils and addresses by student officers, and guest speakers, can do much to arouse enthusiasm among both parents and pupils.

The procedures for arousing interest, recruiting members, and gaining support for the program are important to the choral teacher. Regardless of the music talents and teaching skills of the director, the choral program cannot achieve maximum success unless it is built upon a foundation of enthusiastic cooperation among all concerned. The ultimate success of a choral group is often determined by the teacher's skill in solving problems outside of the rehearsal room.

RECRUITING: INSTRUMENTAL GROUPS

Demonstrations

Perhaps the most successful means of arousing interest in instrumental music is the demonstration. The instrumental teacher first secures the approval of the principal of the school in which instruments of the band and orchestra are to be displayed and demonstrated. It may be an assembly program for the entire school, a similar program for selected pupils, such as those in the fifth grade, or an informal demonstration in one or more classrooms. For the display the teacher selects one of each type of instrument, being especially careful to choose instruments that are in good condition, well shined, and can be displayed to good advantage.

The program itself consists of the display, playing demonstrations of the instruments, remarks concerning their use in bands and orchestras, and interesting sidelights concerning their history. When practical, selections by an instrumental ensemble lend further interest to the program. In most instances it is advantageous to ask competent members of the band or orchestra to demonstrate the instruments. The audience is more interested in the playing of a pupil, and most teachers are not capable of demonstrating all the instruments adequately. The remarks concerning each instrument may be made by the student instrumentalists and supplemented as necessary by the teacher. At some point in the program the teacher explains that instrumental instruction and perhaps the instruments themselves are provided by the school, describes the instrumental program briefly, and invites interested pupils to apply for lessons.

The success of the demonstration stems largely from the children's natural curiosity and the irresistible attractions of shiny instruments. Children, especially those of elementary school age, find it hard to resist the lure of the instruments on display. They want to see them at close range, are curious about the sounds they produce, ask to hold the instruments, to press valves and keys, and even to produce tones. Interest is heightened by the appearance of older pupils as performers and by the presentation of music played by the instruments in various combinations.

An assembly program of this type is usually an unqualified success. If the assembly program is impractical, the teacher can obtain equally satisfactory results by appearing in a classroom with only a few instruments, perhaps trumpet, clarinet, violin, and flute, and with only one or two student instrumentalists to assist him. Although the program is best presented in the elementary school, it is equally effective in the junior high school if limitations of time or equipment do not permit the establishment of an elementary school instrumental program.

If the director of instrumental music wants to establish and maintain a strong orchestra, he should go into the fourth grade with a demonstration of the string instruments before he goes into the fifth grade with the wind instruments. He will need this advantage to overcome the greater attraction of the wind instruments. He should promote the strings with the same energy and enthusiasm as he will the winds. Indeed, the winds will sell themselves. The strings need his most carefully prepared and dynamic sales demonstration.

The children who chose a string instrument in the fourth grade will be in an extremely delicate situation when the fifth-grade demonstration comes along. The novelty of their involvement has worn off; the winds are so much more glamorous and exciting; the excitement in the room seems suddenly to be more than they can bear. They simply must get into the act.

The director should do everything in his power to sustain the young string players through this period of struggle and indecision. He might schedule a concert for the beginning string players on the day of the wind demonstration so that the young string players are not even in the room that day. Or he might close the wind demonstration with a short concert by the string players, thus giving them an instant measure of status and recognition among their peers. Or he might allow some of the string players to start on a wind instrument, but only with the condition that they stay on their string instrument for at least another year.

Somehow, some way, the director must not allow the string program to suffer when the wind demonstration comes along.

Recruiting Through Concerts

As in the choral program, the teacher who wants to stimulate interest in the instrumental program makes it a practice to give regular concerts for the junior high and elementary schools from which new members are recruited. The very nature of the instrumental program gives the instrumental director a greater variety of possibilities for successful recruiting procedures.

A concert can be presented in the junior high school or in the elementary school itself. Or pupils from these schools can be invited to a special concert in the high school auditorium. If the audience is small the concert can be given in the instrumental rehearsal room. This desirable arrangement permits the visitors to see instruments at close range and to become acquainted with "behind-the-scene" rehearsal procedures in an informal atmosphere. Concerts should be short, considerate of the limited attention span of the young audience, and as varied and entertaining as possible. Concert selections are adjusted to the age and interests of the audience, are light and gay in mood, and include special arrangements of familiar and popular songs. Novelties lend interest to the program as does the inclusion of soloists and ensembles.

Because this type of concert is given as part of the recruiting program, the teacher takes full advantage of the opportunity to display and demonstrate the various instruments to the pupils in the audience. He may talk briefly about each instrument, ask a member of the performing group to show his instrument and play a characteristic passage, and point out portions of the concert selections that feature one instrument or a family of instruments. When practical, the audience may be invited to walk through the band or orchestra at the end of the concert to look more closely at the instruments and ask questions. Included in the program is the teacher's invitation to begin instrumental lessons.

On a smaller scale, concerts can be provided for junior high and elementary school pupils by soloists and ensembles that appear in assemblies or individual clasrooms. These concerts offer excellent performance outlet for advanced players from the high school orchestra and band. The practice serves three purposes: it is useful in the recruiting program, gives valuable peforming experience to advanced instrumentalists, and helps improve the music programs of the lower schools. The value to the recruiting program is that it gives pupils in the lower grades close contact with the instruments. The experience of seeing and hearing them at close range in the classroom is far more meaningful and generates stronger interest than seeing them in the relatively formal atmosphere of the auditorium concert. When presenting programs of this sort the student players tell the younger children something about the instruments, demonstrate them, and answer questions asked by the audience. Such programs are supervised by the high school teacher and planned in advance with the cooperation of the teacher responsible for the music work of the lower grade.

Another type of concert is that offered by bands, orchestras, and ensembles from schools of neighboring communities. These are especially useful if it is desired to stimulate the interest of school administrators, parents, or the community. To begin an entirely new instrumental program the appearance of an outstanding group from another school may be all that is required to provide the needed impetus. A concert presented during a school assembly will arouse the interest of the student body. An evening concert may be used to stimulate community enthusiasm. Similar concerts can be arranged if it is desired to improve an existing program or to expand it through the addition of new offerings or organizations.

Pre-band Instruments

To make full use of the interest-arousing possibilities in the regular elementary school program, the high school teacher of instrumental music encourages the use of pre-band or "exploratory" instruments. An organized teaching program including both class lessons and ensemble experience is established for the grade immediately before the one in which the teacher first invites pupils to study band and orchestra instruments. If band instruments are offered in the fifth grade, for example, pre-band instruments are presented to pupils in the fourth grade. Due to the limited progress possible with the simple instruments, one year or less of systematic instruction is sufficient in most instances, the span of instruction being reduced for pupils in the upper elementary grades because they master the instruments quickly and tend to lose interest if the instruction is continued beyond a one-year period.

Pre-band instruments can be taught effectively and economically and can contribute to the success of both elementary school vocal program and the high school instrumental program. Because they are inexpensive, pre-band instruments can be provided for an entire class or for an entire grade including one hundred or more children. In some instances the school bears the entire cost; in others parents make this realtively small expenditure. Because pre-band instruments are simple, children can learn to play them quickly and without the difficulties of embouchure or fingering encountered in wind instruments of the band. And because instruction can be given to large groups, the teacher need not devote a large number of hours to this teaching.

For the instrumental teacher pre-band instruments serve as a fairly reliable indicator of instrumental aptitude and interest. The teacher is usually able to separate easily those who have natural ability from those who have difficulty; the child who is unable to play a pre-band instrument because he is deficient in coordination or rhythmic sense is not a good candidate for further instrumental instruction. In addition, the extended period of instruction separates the pupils who have only transient interest, because of the novelty of the pre-band instrument, from those who want to learn to play and are capable of sustained interest and effort.

It is possible to teach through these instruments skills of value in both instrumental and vocal music. Children gain music-reading skill much more quickly through the instruments than through the vocal program. They learn to finger the instrument, to use the tongue, to provide breath support for the tone, and to play with others in an ensemble. Although children learn less in these areas than is needed to play a band or orchestra instrument, and although they must learn new fingering patterns and embouchure sensations when transferring to other wind instruments, the experience with pre-band instruments gives them an acquaintance with instrumental techniques that makes the initial stage of learning to play another instrument much less difficult.

STUDENT ASSISTANTS

A beginning music teacher often makes the mistake of doing everything that has to be done himself. In his eager concern for ensuring that every item is covered properly and well, he spends countless hours filing music, taking attendance, checking this and that, and dissipating his energy and enthusiasm in all manner of routine clerical tasks. Experienced teachers do not. Experienced teachers assign nearly all routine tasks to student assistants.

By permitting students to assist him in these tasks, and to shoulder certain responsibilities themselves, the music teacher not only frees himself for the musical work which only he can do, but he stimulates student interest and cooperation as well. Adolescent pupils especially want to feel they are accepting adult responsibilities, that they are directing their own efforts with some degree of independence, and that they are respected for their abilities and their opinions. The teacher caters to these normal adolescent desires by delegating some of his duties to student assistants and by adopting democratic procedures for the nonmusical phases of the music program. By doing so he creates opportunity for outstanding pupils to provide the enthusiastic participation of which they are capable.

One means of providing this assistance is through the establishment of parliamentary organization in the ensemble. Once each year, or more often if necessary, the group nominates and elects officers, determines needed committees, and discusses the duties of each office. Thereafter it holds meetings as necessary to conduct the business of the organization. A president and secretary are needed, and other officers such as treasurer, business manager, and publicity manager may be elected or appointed as necessary. Certain posts must of necessity be filled by appointment, the teacher selecting pupils who have the abilities required of the several needed accompanists, assistant conductor, librarians, equipment manager, section leaders, and other special assistants.

Committees may be elected by the group. A membership committee is helpful in planning and carrying out the annual recruiting drive and the publicity that precedes it. If the chorus is in demand for out-of-school performances a steering or program committee can evaluate all performance requests, handle related corespondence, and make transportation and other arrangements for concert appearances. A social committee is sometimes desirable to discuss the possibilities of an annual dance, picnic, or other activity, to make plans, secure extra pupil assistance, and arrange for details. The possibilities for this sort of organization are almost limitless. There are pitfalls for the teacher, of course, if the multiplicity of officers and activities converts the ensemble from a musical to a social organization, requiring that rehearsal time be given up to business meetings and committee discussions. Further, there is the ever-present possibility that elections determine who is popular rather than who is best qualified for each post. With proper guidance, however, the student organization can become indispensable to the teacher as a means of bringing systematic order to the hundreds of scattered nonmusical administrative necessities involved in the efficient operation of a large performing ensemble.

The teacher should not hesitate to be a bit authoritarian with his student assistants. It should be clearly understood by all that if a student assistant fails to carry out his responsibilities he will be replaced, without malice, by someone who will do the job. Even with elected officers the teacher should make it quite clear to all that he reserves the right to call for a new election if critical duties are not being handled efficiently and effectively. To balance his dictatorial posture here, the teacher should be certain to give proper credit to his staff of assistants in printed concert programs, newspaper articles, and in the school yearbook. The combined effect of this carrot-and-stick approach will usually keep things running smoothly.

PROPERTY MANAGEMENT AND BUDGETS

A music department must acquire large quantities of expensive equipment to achieve its educational goals. Instruments, uniforms, robes, risers, music folders, printed music, music stands, storage cabinets, and many other necessities increase the required music department investment to a sum larger than that required by most other school departments. All this equipment must be purchased, maintained, and properly accounted for at all times. The burden of work is large enough to consume nearly all the teacher's time if he does not manage it systematically. With careful planning, this work can be accomplished quickly and efficiently and with great benefit to the general development of the music program.

The Music Budget

The music budget is a systematic approach to the financial problems of the music department. It can deal with instrumental music alone, with all performing groups in one school, both vocal and instrumental, or with the entire music program from grade one through grade twelve. The ideal budget is one that functions effectively year after year, retaining the same basic framework but permitting revision of minor details to compensate for the growth of the music program or other special circumstances. Advance planning is essential. Music department needs must be known in advance so a place for them can be reserved in the total school budget. Advance planning is further required because school funds must be obtained and set aside long before they are spent. Finally, the music director plans in terms of the school population, estimating years in advance the effect increases in enrollment will have on instrument classes and advanced performing groups. Budgeted amounts depend therefore upon the size of classes and performing groups, the importance of music in the school program, and, of course, the amount of money available through normal channels of school revenue.

Budget Categories

In formulating a budget it is helpful to establish broad categories of expenditure. Each category is considered separately in terms of its relative importance in the total budget, the amount of funds it requires, and the frequency of its occurrence. Certain new equipment such as instruments, robes, or uniforms requires extraordinary expenditure, either a large special appropriation once every several years or regular small appropriations annually. The occasional large appropriation is advantageous in that it sometimes permits the economies of quantity purchase and permits the school to acquire simultaneously a large number of items of the same make, model, and quality. The smaller annual appropriation is usually preferred, however, because it spreads the expenditure evenly over many years instead of burdening the budget in any one year. Funds for maintenance and repair are needed every year, are spent as needed, and may be among the largest items in the budget. Other items may be irregular, such as special music and scenery for special shows. Budget needs for these items are determined far in advance and orders placed with suppliers before their seasonal rush.

A list of possible categories is shown here as an indication of needs that might be common to all music departments. The items in each category are examples only and do not show the total range of needed materials and equipment.

1. *Instructional materials:* textbooks, band, choir, and orchestra arrangements, ensemble pieces, method books, rehearsal folders, librarian's supplies.
2. *Expendable supplies:* bond, carbon, and onionskin paper, music manuscript paper, mimeograph stencils, chalk, answer sheets for standardized tests, recording tapes.
3. *Instructional equipment:* phonograph, tape recorder, electronic tuning devices, music stands, special rehearsal chairs.
4. *Instructional expenses:* film rental, performance cost including program printing, concert hall rental, janitorial fees.
5. *School equipment:* storage cabinets for instruments, music, robes, and uniforms, rehearsal room risers, phonograph records, duplicating machines.
6. *Maintenance and repair:* instrument repair and replacement, uniform and robe cleaning, repair, and replacement, piano tuning, purchase of tools for instrument repairs.
7. *Capital outlay:* purchase of instruments, robes, and uniforms.
8. *Insurance:* protection against damage, loss, and fire for instruments, robes, uniforms, and other equipment; liability insurance covering injury to pupils during trips or any out-of-school function.
9. *Miscellaneous and contingency:* festival expenses, including registration fees, transportation, housing and meals; purchase of extra reeds, mouthpieces, and other small supplies.

Submitting Requests for Funds

There are a number of principles to be observed when preparing budget requests for the approval of administrative officers. Requests must be businesslike in every detail. They are prepared in written form, brief, but with all necessary information included. They are organized logically, showing the need for funds, being considerate of necessary limitations placed upon expenditure, giving accurate figures for current requests, and showing how major improvements can be achieved through long-range planning. Finally, they include any information needed to justify expenditures or to help the administrator form conclusions concerning the relative importance of separate items.

The allocation of school funds is a major responsibility of administrative officers and a time-consuming portion of their work. Because the administrator's time is limited, budget requests are submitted in a form that permits quick initial scanning, detailed later study, conventional filing, and subsequent reference. The administrator respects and is sympathetic toward the music director whose budget requests show careful organization. They save time for the administrator and are evidence of good judgment in the preparation of the budget and the expenditure of school funds. For this reason the music director who follows businesslike principles in preparing his budget can be confident of its approval whenever the school budget permits.

The written budget request might consist of the following:

1. *General statement.* Identifies the department submitting the budget and the period covered, requests special consideration of specific items as necessary, and may state briefly selected facts about goals or needs.
2. *Budget synopsis.* A brief summary of budget requests by major categories suitable for quick scanning and easy reference.
3. *Specific requests.* This is the body of the budget request. It lists all categories of expenditure, states amounts desired, gives costs, discounts, purchase specifications, sources, and the like.
4. *Supplementary information.* Contains any information useful to the administrative officer, including (a) description of current needs, (b) enrollment figures and trends, (c) plans for additional classes or performing groups, (d) long-range plans, (e) comparative bids, (f) alternate sources.

THE MUSIC LIBRARY: CHORAL MUSIC

If he aspires to variety and vitality in his work, the director of choral music must know precisely what music is available to him in his library at all times. At a moment's notice he should be able to determine how many copies he has of any given composition by any given composer, and in what voicing and accompaniment the work is set. He needs what might be called a director's personal library.

During the first few weeks before school opens, therefore, a new choral director will do well to go through the entire choral library, extracting one good copy of each piece of music, each anthology, each item for the groups he will direct. He should mark this copy with whatever mark will lead him straight to the file drawer or shelf location of the work. He should also indicate the number of copies which exist for each item. He will then have, in numerical or alphabetical or whatever order, a miniature version of the school's entire choral library—complete with information on the number of copies available and usable.

Next, he should prepare a 3 x 5 inch card index of this information: composition, library number, composer or arranger, voicing, number of copies, and remarks on the irregularity of accompaniment setting, if any. He should then prepare another 3 x 5 inch card index, a cross index by composer. This index may contain only the composer's name and the name of the composition, and perhaps the dates of past performances as far back as can be determined with assuredness.

During the first few days of the new school year the choir secretary and choir librarians should prepare a duplicate of each index, one set of indexes to be kept at the director's home or in his school office, or wherever he does his professional planning, the other set of indexes to be kept in the choir rehearsal area readily available to the choir librarians.

When the indexes are complete and up-to-date, the choir director can sit down to plan his work with intelligence and good musical judgment. Several important considerations may come to light. He may discover that the library is alarmingly short on works by first-rate composers. In a typical school library there may well be precious few works by Josquin, Palestrina, Bach, Handel, Mozart, Mendelssohn, Brahms, Thompson, Britten, and others who have contributed to the history and development of choral music. Or he may discover that the choir has not done a composition by Brahms in the last five years or so. Or he may discover three motets by Vittoria that have never been done. Or he may discover that a small body of relatively substantial music has been done over and over again during the past few years.

Whatever he discovers, it will be specific information. As such, it will be more revealing to him than the casual impressions he has gathered from program notes and from sincere but nonprofessional observations of students, parents, and school officials. With this kind of specific information at his fingertips the director can make immediate and long-range preparations to build the library in its weak areas, to dig out first-rate music from style periods which have not been touched for awhile, and to bring an overall sense of purpose and direction to the day-by-day and year-by-year choral activities of the school and the community.

THE MUSIC LIBRARY: INSTRUMENTAL MUSIC

The director of instrumental music has a considerably more elaborate music library to get organized. Efficient management of this library requires a large number of records and the constant attention of an industrious librarian. There are many possible systems for filing band and orchestra music, but the following items are required in almost any system:

1. *Library file cards.* Cards are purchased in sets of four so that each band or orchestra selection can be indexed under (a) composer, (b) title, (c) character, (d) file number. Each card of the set is a different color and is arranged so that the important indexing item appears on the top line. One card contains detailed information about the selection —composer, title, arranger, file number, character, publisher, publisher's catalog number, cost, performance dates. The other three cards of each set contain only the information needed for cross-reference. Cards of the same color are filed together, each color in its own file drawer.

2. *File envelopes.* Envelopes, folders, or boxes are needed to protect the music stored in drawers or cabinets. Envelopes, preferred by many directors, can be purchased in march, octavo, and concert sizes. The face of each envelope provides spaces to show (a) file number, (b) composer, (c) title, (d) arranger, (e) character, (f) publisher, (g) cost, (h) parts list, (i) performance dates, (j) remarks. The parts list is especially important. It permits the librarian to check the instrumentation and number of copies of each part without opening the envelope.

3. *Concert folders.* Folders are necessary to protect music, prevent loss of individual parts, and simplify issue and return of music at rehearsal. They are made of heavy stock or hardboard with inner pockets to hold parts and may have envelope flaps. The chief requisites are that they be made of sturdy material and constructed so that music cannot fall out when the folder is closed.

4. *March folders.* Special folders of march size are provided for each member of the marching band. The folder consists of plastic pockets hinged together for easy turning. Music placed inside the pockets is protected from rain and other damage but visible through the plastic face. Folders can be placed in music lyres and pages turned easily, the hinge preventing loss of parts on the march.

5. *Sign-out sheets.* One sheet is provided for each concert folder so that players can leave the sheet with the librarian whenever a folder is taken from the rehearsal room for individual practice. Each sheet shows (a) concert folder number, (b) instrument, (c) stand number, (d) date issued, (e) student signature, (f) date returned, (g) librarian's signature.

6. *Music order blank.* These blanks are for the convenience of the director in ordering band and orchestra selections. The director types three copies—for the supplier, the school office, and his own file—or more if the school purchasing system requires. The form provides headings for (a) supplier's name and address, (b) school name and address, (c) school order number, (d) title of selection, (e) composer,

(f) arranger, (g) publisher, (h) publisher's catalog number, (i) list price, (j) discount, (k) parts list, (l) music director's signature and title. The parts list is particularly useful because it permits the director to order standard, symphonic, or other sets of parts plus as many extra parts as needed for his performing group.

The following equipment other than printed forms and folders is of use to the librarian:

1. *Sorting rack.* This is an arrangement of shelves providing space for the display of each concert folder separately. Shelves are tipped forward so that all folders are visible and parts can be distributed by placing each part on its proper folder.

2. *Folder file.* A cabinet containing shelves or slots, each labeled to receive one concert folder. Players select their own folders before rehearsal and replace them in the proper slots at the end of each rehearsal.

3. *Work table.* A large table providing ample working surface and drawer space for storage is useful to the librarian for sorting, mending music, cataloging, and so forth.

The most convenient receptacle for file cards is a multidrawer cabinet. Single wood or steel drawers can be used as the library is being developed and when the number of file cards is small, but the expanding library quickly requires additional drawers. Band and orchestra arrangements can be stored in several ways. (1) Sliding-drawer file cabinets are practical and require that each selection be placed in its own envelope. (2) Selections can be placed in file boxes of heavy cardboard, each selection in its own box and the boxes placed like books on library shelves. (3) Another possibility, suitable for temporary use until filing equipment can be purchased, is the "lay-away" system. Each selection is placed in its own file folder, the spine of the folder is labeled, and the folders are piled on shelves in file order. Of all the possibilities, sliding-drawer cabinets are preferred by many directors because they protect the music fully, occupy relatively little space, and permit easy access.

Although the use of four file cards for each selection helps determine categories for filing, it is sometimes useful to establish additional categories to govern placement of selections in file drawers. Categories might include chorales, marches, novelties, overtures, popular selections, sacred music, solos with full accompaniment, suites, symphonic excerpts, and so forth. All marches are filed together in special drawers of march size. Other selections can be grouped in standard drawers so that all selections of each type are filed together. If this is done, each category is identified by a file-number prefix and each selection by the prefix plus the file number. Chorales, for example, would be numbered C-1, C-2, and so on.

Of more importance is the numbering of parts to prevent loss and as an aid in filing. When new music is received, parts are arranged in score order, numbers are entered in the parts list on the face of the envelope, and the parts are placed in the envelope in score order. In addition, each part is numbered, the numbers indicating score order, the number of copies of each part, and the concert folder in which each part is to be placed. The simplest way is to place parts in score order and number them consecutively, but this prevents the addition of extra parts at a later date. A more elaborate but practical method is to assign a block of numbers of each part as in Table 1, reserving unused numbers for later addition of extra parts.

If this system is followed, the first flute part will always be number 1, first cornet number 100, first baritone number 140. Concert folders are then given the same numbers so that part number 1 is always placed in folder number 1. To distribute music the librarian places concert folders on the sorting rack in numerical order and places a part of the correct number on each folder. Parts are removed from the folders in a similar manner, and a missing part can be identified by its number, showing which folder is incomplete and which player is responsible. Collected parts are then piled in numerical order, the quantities of each part checked against the parts list on the file envelope, and the complete selection filed in correct order ready for redistribution when needed.

GUIDELINES FOR PROFESSIONALISM

The preceding suggestions for specific circumstances leave hundreds of items unaccounted for. This must be. Each teaching situation involves a host of subtle and complex administrative problems peculiar to that situation. A few general guidelines for new teachers, whatever the situation, may be of interest.

First, be patient, persistent, professional. At their root, administrative problems are often more than mere problems of finances, procedures, or logistics; they are problems of getting human beings—students, parents, colleagues, school officials—to see the need for certain conditions. When human beings cluster into social units—parent clubs, student bodies, teaching staffs, administrative organizations—they tend to get a little conservative, as a group, at least. A new music teacher, therefore, cannot expect to realize his fondest dreams overnight. He must gather his evidence and present it to the people involved, and then patiently give all parties time to reflect on the matter. If nothing develops the first time around, the teacher should not hesitate in the least to inquire again, after a reasonable period, as to the probability of his request being answered.

TABLE 1

Suggested Numbering System for Parts in Band Arrangements

Number	Parts	Number	Parts
1–9	Flutes and piccolos	90–94	Bass saxophones
10–14	Oboes and English horns	100–109	Cornets
15–19	E-flat clarinets	110–114	Trumpets
20–49	B-flat clarinets	115–119	Fluegelhorns
50–54	Alto clarinets	120–129	French horns
55–59	Bass clarinets	130–139	Trombones
60–64	Contra-bass clarinets	140–149	Baritones
65–69	Bassoons	150–159	Tubas
70–74	Soprano saxophones	160–164	String basses
75–79	Alto saxophones	200–209	Percussion
80–84	Tenor saxophones	210–214	Harps
85–89	Baritone saxophones		

A reasonable period may be two weeks or a year. If a new teacher is consistent and persistent, and if his evidence is convincing, there is every good reason to believe that the wisdom of his position will eventually prevail. Whether or not he gets what he wants, he must at all times be completely professional in his relations with those around him. Win, lose, or draw, there should be no indignant "letters to the editor," no unsolicited remarks to or about associates, no lamentations about or among the students.

Second, follow the chain-of-command. Take requests to immediate superiors, and be certain to inform these immediate superiors if a higher authority is already informed of the request or, possibly, will be informed of the request. Equally important, take the request to immediate superiors at the proper time. The biweekly Monday afternoon teachers' meeting is not the time to bear down on the principal for new choir robes.

Third, put the music program in its proper perspective. If a fine young trumpet player is failing English and algebra, the English teacher and algebra teacher have first claim on his time and energy. Students who are failing in academic studies should not be permitted to perform in public. Holding to this rule may be painful, even disastrous, the first few times, but in the long-range scheme of things the rule will improve the overall quality and prestige of the music program.

Fourth, make every effort to cooperate with service personnel. Custodians, bus drivers, and maintenance men very properly look upon the music program as only one part of their total responsibility to the school system. They are usually quite willing to accommodate the music teacher in all reasonable demands. All they ask is time to prepare for extra responsibilities and an honest word of thanks when the project is done.

A music teacher will do himself and the music program a great service, then, if he works hard at handling administrative necessities in an unassuming, professional manner. No need to be unduly officious, no need to be artificially humble. Just do the job that has to be done, and go at it with emotional restraint, intelligent application, and good-natured industry—and with a genuine concern for the related needs of all parties involved.

► CHAPTER 6

Rehearsal Procedures

Public school performing organizations spend nearly all their time
rehearsing. Day after day, week after week, they labor dutifully to
improve their collective technique and to enlarge their concert repertoire.
After several months of rehearsal the groups make a formal public appearance—of near-professional quality, often—returning to the rehearsal
room, then, for several more months of preparation. As a rule, two large-
scale formal concerts are prepared each year, one near the Christmas
season, the other near the end of the school year in April or May.
Shorter, somewhat more informal public apearances are scattered
throughout the year, but the selections for these shorter public appearances are usually drawn from among the selections prepared for the
large concert appearances.

In the professional world such "rehearsal groups" spring up, now
and then, among jazz performers locked in the security of steady work in
commercial dance bands and, more and more these days, among lovers
and players of chamber music lost in the crowded ranks of symphony
orchestra sections. In the amateur world the city band and the civic
orchestra stand as a rough parallel to the public school performing organizations in matters of rehearsal-to-performance ratios, general difficulty of the repertoire, and overall sociomusical function. But even here
the public school groups enjoy quite an advantage in the regularity, frequency, and total number of rehearsals that go into each performance.

All factors considered, the public school performing ensemble is a truly unique and typically American phenomenon, and, should it never make a public appearance, the ensemble would still serve a valid educational and musical end.

The large ensemble in the secondary schools is best described, perhaps, as a study group—a group which meets regularly to study a given body of the music of Western civilization. The music is studied in the most direct manner possible: performance by those studying. Rehearsals, then, are really music lessons, and should be planned with the same care as any other music lesson. Rehearsals are also lecture-demonstrations on music by the music director for the students. And to some extent rehearsals are concertlike living experiences in music for the members of the ensembles.

REHEARSAL PREPARATION

This multiplicity of functions which falls to the rehearsal of a public school performing ensemble need not trouble a new music teacher in the least. If he sets out carefully to make each rehearsal an efficient, productive, and genuine musical experience for all concerned, the philosophical issues will take care of themselves. At the risk of oversimplification, four principles of rehearsal preparation are offered herewith.

First, choose quality music. No amount of strenuous preparation will make a bad piece of music worth the effort. A young teacher should probably stay with name composers until he finds his way around the medium and its literature. Very important, get a recording of the composition if at all possible. Many of the large colleges and schools of music are recording public school band, choir, and orchestra contest music these days to augment the standard commercial offerings. A new director should look into the possibility of subscribing to these special recordings. A new director might also call the director of the neighboring high school ensemble or the director of a college group in the vicinity to see if either of them might have a tape recording of the composition. There is no real urgency, of course, if the work is very simple and if its interpretation is fairly restricted by the technical limitations of the ensemble. In a more complex piece of music, though, the industrious new music director should do everything in his power to unearth a recorded version of the work to help him prepare his rehearsals.

Second, get a full score to the music. If the composition is something that the director will do many times in his career, he might buy a clothbound full score for his own professional conductor's library. If no full score is available—as sometimes happens with compositions for band—he should make one from the parts. The experience will be a superb lesson in transposition intervals, idiomatic part-writing, and general scoring techniques. It may take nine or ten hours to make a full score. But the score is going to be used periodically over the next thirty to forty years, and it is surely not unreasonable to expect a young conductor to make this kind of investment in his professional career.

The full score should be studied as carefully as a scientist studies a slide under a microscope. The instrumental parts, or the accompaniment part, or whatever other items go to make up the entire musical operation should be at hand during this initial study of the full score. In even the most carefully edited music, rehearsal numbers will be misplaced, phrase marks will not agree, and an occasional accidental will be omitted. These irregularities should be caught before the music is handed out to the youngsters.

Of greater instructional import than merely correcting a misplaced rehearsal number is the director's conscientious marking of standard and alternate fingerings, proper bowings, regular and substitute slide positions, articulation patterns, and interpretation adjustments in the students' parts and in his own conductor's score. This is a time-consuming job, but if it is done once, properly and carefully, it will serve generations of young musicians year after year in the future. There is really no other way to fully appreciate what a student encounters in the music than to play through each part, vicariously, with pencil in hand, marking things that are confusing or troublesome. The beginning conductor will probably need a book of fingering charts at his side to do the job with any confidence. After a dozen scores or so, however, things will run along fairly smoothly.

The choral conductor's task in score preparation is less rigorous and involved, but it must still be done. He should sing through each part, in tempo, with the words. He may want to put an arrow pointing up, perhaps, over notes that must be lifted—leading tones, major thirds, and nearly all notes altered in an upward direction. Likewise, he may want to put an arrow pointing down over notes that must be lowered in pitch —minor sevenths, fourths, and nearly all notes altered in a downward direction. He might also put in breath marks, adjustments in dynamics, indications for *divisi* procedures, vowel-color suggestions, and whatever other marks will aid the student vocalist.

In his own score the beginning conductor should mark important cues and significant musical events several measures in advance of the time he will want to make the cue or press for emphasis of the musical event. Some kind of warning sign in measure 14, for example, will call his attention to the important subtheme in the violoncellos at measure 17. Merely marking measure 17 is often not enough for young conductors just learning to read full scores.

All of this work, marking parts and scores and checking one against other, demands time and energy that the beginning conductors might want to put elsewhere. Should he not have his section leaders, accompanist, assistant conductor, or principal instrumentalists do this work? Probably not. At least not during the first year or two of his career. There is no training in the world more valuable to a new director than to learn, firsthand, exactly what goes on below the surface sights and sounds of his band, choir, or orchestra. Furthermore, a director's first six months of rehearsals are crucially habit-forming. If these rehearsals go smoothly and efficiently because of his total command of the situation, with parts and score in complete presence of mind, the young conductor establishes a professional behavior that will carry him well as the years go by. Like other modes of behavior, excellence can become a habit.

Third, practice. Practice conducting the music in front of a mirror. Work out the specific manner of giving each cue and handling each tempo gradation. Determine exactly how every subtle nuance of the music will be treated. Practice with a music stand properly adjusted, with a metronome to check tempo marks, with the full score already prepared, with a recording near at hand as a point of reference. Go through difficult passages in different ways to find the best conducting manner for each passage. Go through the entire composition several times. Get everything in complete control before the first rehearsal.

Fourth, make a tape recording of every rehearsal for several months. No need for anything special; just turn the machine on at the beginning of the rehearsal and let it run through the entire hour, intermission breaks and all. Study the tapes to determine if comments and instructions are always clear and if corrections are being made efficiently and accurately. How much time do the youngsters actually rehearse each hour? How much time do they spend listening to their director talk? Are the boys and girls performing as well as their director seems to think? From a strictly objective point of view, how does this music and its performance hold up with the outside musical world?

Public school music directors want so desperately to hear things going well in the ranks of their ensembles that they sometimes develop what might be called a "public school ear." They have worked so hard at the job, and their students are trying so valiantly, and the whole town is so thrilled at the progress to date, and the school officials are so pleased with the splendid spirit this year, and the group sounds so improved over their early rehearsals in September—all these factors may lead the director to an unrealistic judgment about the ensemble. His ear may actually deceive him. A tape recording will serve as an important, impartial point of reference. He will hear many things that still need attention, but he will also hear many things that are going well. He should be aware, always, of both. His professional growth depends, to a great extent, on this capacity for continual, honest self-appraisal.

All this preparation and practice may sound a bit ego-centered and specious. It is. It should be. A young music educator who seeks a career as a director of an ensemble should approach his first few rehearsals as an aspiring operatic soprano approaches her grand debut. No amount of careful planning is spared. Nothing is unaccounted for. Ten to fifteen years of study goes on the line. A life-time career is unfolding here, and no circumstance is too insignificant to be given some thought before the big moment.

REHEARSAL DESIGN

Once the conductor decides upon his rehearsal program, he prepares a written lesson like that of the classroom teacher. The conductor's plan includes the sequence of rehearsal activities, special devices or procedures for emphasis of the knowledge to be learned, and notes concerning passages needing special practice. It is written in the form of a timed schedule of events. The estimation of time is essential. It permits the conductor to fill the rehearsal hour with productive work, prevents him from scheduling more work than can be done in one rehearsal, and improves the tempo of his teaching. After each rehearsal the conductor notes on his plan any comments of use to him as he prepares for subsequent rehearsals. He then files each plan for future reference. Depending upon the skill and experience of the conductor, the plan may be either a full sheet of detailed notations or a card bearing little more than titles of selections and the measure numbers identifying sections for intensive practice. In either case the plan itself is a necessity, and few conductors are successful in rehearsal without it.

As in all class-method instruction, routine saves time, variety increases interest, and the cardinal rule is to talk little and play much. Rehearsals usually follow a fairly predictable design. The following order is common:

1. Warm-up routine.
2. Technique-building studies.
3. Performance of a familiar work.

4. Practice on compositions under preparation and, possibly, introducing a new piece of music.
5. Sight-reading experience.
6. Closing performance of another familiar work.

The Warm-up Routine

Musicians young and old need a warm-up period to get prepared for the work of the rehearsal. The need is partly physical, partly psychological. The body and the mind must be put in a state of relaxed attention for the job at hand. Professional musicians know how to warm up; youngsters seldom do. Adolescents look upon the warm-up period as a time for unbridled exhibitionism. As a general rule, a public school music director should permit very little time for free warm-up activities. It is best, all the way around, if he gets complete control of things the moment the boys and girls come through the door of the rehearsal room.

Each director seems to have his own pattern for warming up and his own set of materials. Whatever the variations on the basic theme, two factors must be considered, the instruments and the students. For choir directors the instruments and the students are inseparable, of course, but there may be some virtue in thinking of warming and tuning the "vocal instrument," and in asking the youngsters to try to think along the same line. Choir directors should strive for resonance, proper placement, diaphragmatic support, a spinning tone, relaxed throat and jaw conditions, and a sense of buoyant energy in the choir's overall tone. All manner and variety of devices are employed to get these desiderata. "Mi-me-ma-mo-mu," "hung," "ha-ha-ha-ha," vocalises, scales and chords on neutral syllables, modulating cadential passages, and similar devices are found in abundance. The specific patterns are probably not as crucial as the serious manner of their use and the genuine rehearsal readiness resulting therefrom.

For instrumental directors the instruments and the students are obviously separate items. The job here is to reduce that line of separation—to bring to the instrumentalist the same kind of immediacy with his instrument as exists with the vocalist and his instrument. Instrumental directors should strive for dead-center tuning to an absolute standard, for acceptable tolerances around that absolute standard, for diaphragmatic support, for digital relaxation, for proper embouchure formation, for bow-arm freedom and control, for solid tone production, and for razor-sharp reflexes. Diatonic and chromatic scales, choralelike chord sequences, arpeggios, rhythm drills, and exercises in dynamics control are used singly and in combination by different directors on different occasions. Whatever the devices and materials, the warm-up must be approached by director and students alike in a most intense and serious manner.

Building Technique

A director must set out to build technique in his ensemble just as he would build technique on his own instrument. In a very real sense the ensemble has become the director's performing instrument. To build technique on the instrument the director must practice the things he cannot do on the instrument. Many new music directors get confused here, unknowingly, and fall into a rehearsal routine in which the ensemble seldom tries things it cannot do; there is thus no systematic building of the ensemble's technical prowess.

A new director may spend ten minutes with his string orchestra going through the D-major scale and G-major scale in various bowings and rhythmic patterns. At the end of the ten-minute period he moves into something else thinking he has covered the first two items in his rehearsal order, the warm-up routine and the technique-building drill. He has not. He has warmed up the group. Before the period began the orchestra knew quite well the finger patterns, the bow-arm weight and speed, and all the rest for executing the director's prescribed routine. He has only solidified their technique; he has not built, that is, enlarged, their technical equipment.

Band directors often make the same kind of error. They play the concert B-flat and E-flat major scales in various articulation patterns and rhythms, then move to something else with the feeling that they have built technique. They have not. Choir directors, likewise, with their special patterns, seldom go at the job of building technique in a systematic and productive manner. As a result, a large ensemble's collective facility—the technical equipment of the director's performing instrument: band, choir, or orchestra—really does not exist except as a disjointed compendium of the musical dexterity of the section leaders or principal instrumentalists in the group.

In the professional world an ensemble has a technique of its own which is separate from the aggregate facility of the individual members of the ensemble. The Philadelphia Orchestra or the Robert Shaw Chorale, for example, has a technique which is really the technique of the conductor on his performing instrument, the ensemble. Individual members come and go, but the ensemble always has that special technique, and sound, and musical personality of its own. Indeed, the conductor makes a guest appearance with a completely foreign ensemble, and that foreign

ensemble instantly takes on some of the characteristic traits of the conductor's personal technique.

Public school conductors should give some thought to this rather
esoteric consideration. Otherwise, their band, or choir, or orchestra, will
sound and perform just like everyone else's band, or choir, or orchestra.
There may be no real virtue in trying to sound and perform unlike others,
but the thought of building his own special technique on his own special
performing instrument will lead a new conductor to do some things that
he might not otherwise have done.

If a band director is concerned that he cannot play in the sharp
keys on his instrument, for example, he should take immediate steps to
correct the situation. Next Monday he might ask his band to play—ever
so slowly, in tied whole notes, perhaps—the concert B-major scale. The
shock will send the youngsters scurrying and digging for their fingering
charts. The band director has begun to build technique on his performing instrument.

If a choir director is concerned that he cannot sight-read on his
instrument, for example, he should do something about the situation.
Next Monday he might bring in those thirty-four copies of the old second-
grade *Music Hour* textbooks that the elementary school had in its storage
room, pass the books out to his choir, and sing one or two of the little
tunes each rehearsal until further notice. He should have the choir sing
the tunes first in unison-octaves on a neutral "loo." Then with numbers,
then with syllables, then with words in a beautifully blended, pure,
a cappella delivery. The choir members may think their director is playing games with them. There are sure to be some laughs about the quaint
little tunes and some harmless nonsense with the numbers and syllables.
The director need only stick to his businesslike manner to see the thing
through to its reasonable end. He knows, and the students will later
realize, that choral technique is being built here.

If a director of a string orchestra is concerned that his instrument
is always a little unsteady in flat keys, he should not avoid the flat keys.
Rather, he should jump into flats at every convenient turn. Why not have
the youngsters play the D-flat major scale, for example, while warming
up the bow arm? Or if he is concerned that his instrument, the string
orchestra, is always a bit disjointed, with no sense of precision and co-
hesion, he should take immediate steps to do something about this im-
perfection of technique. Next Monday he might ask the orchestra to play
a scale, four quarter notes on each pitch, pizzicato, eyes closed, following
only the concertmaster's sound. The concertmaster should take slight
liberties with the tempo, at his pleasure. Nothing too extreme, just the
kind of give-and-take that might ordinarily occur in the unfolding of

traditional melodic materials. Unorthodox as this may be, the orchestra director is building technique. He is bringing refinement to his performing skill on his instrument, the orchestra.

A warm-up routine is one thing; building technique is another. Building technique requires continual, often uncomfortable expansion and extension of proficiencies. The best way to expand and extend technical proficiency is to spend a few of the precious moments of each rehearsal in exercises designed specifically to do just that: to build technique.

Performance of a Familiar Work

There is nothing to belabor here. Just perform the composition with full and proper attention to all details. No stopping, even though something is not exactly comfortable. No comments, even though a few things are in need of correction. Make this a genuine musical experience for the group. The overriding concern at this point is not instruction but the exhilarating joy of making music. There should be a few of these moments in each rehearsal; this is one of them.

Working on Compositions Under Preparation

Before the rehearsal the director has isolated the areas that need work in the compositions under preparation. There is no need to work up to, or around, or past the areas. Go right to the difficult area, and dig in. Take it one musical component at a time in reduced tempo. Take it in functional units, the rhythmic group pitted against the melodic group. Take it vertically, eighth note at a time. Take it backwards. Yes, take it in reverse, eighth note at a time. Take it nearly up to tempo. Take it at the desired tempo. Take it faster than it will ever be performed. Remove all dots from the dotted rhythms. Put dots on all equal rhythms. Take it *fortissimo*. Take it *pianissimo*. Take it *legato*. Take it *staccato*. Take it every other way except the way it is often taken, over-and-over-and-over again.

Try to avoid, "Cellos, may I hear you at 12 after C, please." Better: "Everyone except cellos 'loo-loo-loo' his notes, and move his fingers on his instrument, please. Here we go, 12 after C." Try to avoid, "Tenors, may I hear you from A to B, please." Better: "Let us all sing the tenor part from A to B, please. Tenors sing the words; choir sings 'la-la-la.'" Try to avoid, "Mary, play the alto part at letter G, please. Altos, listen." Better: "Choir, sing at G, please. Piano, play only the alto line. Altos, hum very quietly, listening to how your notes 'feel' in the music. Choir, sing in the normal manner."

Try to avoid, "Third clarinets, may I hear you at measure 26." Better to ask the solo clarinetist (already preenrolled at a fine music school for the next academic year): "John, would you bring your A clarinet to rehearsal until further notice, please. I want you to play the third clarinet part with the section every now and then. You will have to transpose for yourself while you help them get their fingerings and pitches. It will be good experience for you and for them. All clarinet chairs are frozen until John helps us out for the next few rehearsals."

Every director has his own method of bringing a composition up to concert readiness. As a jockey paces a race horse, a music director must pace the ensemble so that the youngsters arrive at the concert date in full enthusiasm and preparedness. Too much preparation too soon will result in a preconcert slump. Too little too late will be equally disastrous. The fine art of bringing everything to a peak on the day of the concert is one that must be learned by trial and error by each music director for himself. After the first few concerts he will have some notion as to what works best for him with his groups. From then on it is simply a matter of careful control, constant checking, and a bit of good luck.

Introducing a New Composition

Plunging into a new composition for the first time is, likewise, an art that must be learned empirically. If a recording is available, the first step should be for the students to hear the recording, music in front of them, before they play a note. If a recording is not available, the first step should be to go straight through the composition without lengthy comments about the composer, the style, the theme, and all the other things of interest. Save these little items to insert throughout the coming rehearsals when the embouchures and ears need a moment's rest. In this initial reading the director will have to call out numbers, sing melodies not being offered, call out metric stresses, tap out the rhythmic patterns, and push, encourage, and pull the group through the generality of the musical experience. At best the group will have only a vague notion about the real musical experience which lies on the page before them. Suffice for the moment.

Then take a structural unit, and dig in at a tempo so slow that everyone can get all the notes, complete with words, or articulations, or bowings, and complete with interpretive expression in all its complexities: balance, blend, phrasing, dynamics, rubato passages—the full musical offering. What gradually takes shape, then, from the very first rehearsal, is a composition performed with its essential components being delivered accurately every time. The only component waiting to be developed is the tempo. Tempo is, to be sure, one of the most crucial factors; thus, this technique of preparing a new composition has this limitation. A march is just not a march at one-sixth proper speed. It is not as bad as might be expected, though, when all other stylistic elements are observed faithfully.

Limitations notwithstanding, this technique has the sovereign virtue of preventing the youngsters from getting off to a bad start on a new piece of music. Let a student musician deliver a passage out of style, with a wrong note or two, for the first week of his contact with the music, and it will take several weeks to break the bad habit and several more weeks to establish the correct habit. Then—and here is the most frustrating part —at the moment in the public concert when that particular passage is to be performed, if the student is extra nervous or caught off guard for any reason, the original erroneous passage may emerge again, strong and clear as ever. This strange power of original contact is a most curious aspect of music learning. Because first contact is so strong, many directors forbid their students to practice a new composition except under guidance in the early stages of preparing the composition. And some class-method instructors keep the instruments in the classroom for the first few weeks of a beginning class for the same reason.

Far too much of any music teacher's work seems to be breaking bad habits that should not have developed in the beginning. Oddly enough the young music director often allows these habits to develop right in front of him because his attention is seemingly more properly applied elsewhere. All in all, a new director should give as much time and energy to precluding the incorrect response as he does to eliciting the correct response when leading his ensemble into a new musical experience.

Sight-Reading

There is no real problem here. Just do it. Get very easy music to start out with, and do one or two complete compositions at the beginning of the rehearsal at a tempo quite slower than usual. The strategy is to make the notation so easy, and the tempo so slow, that even the least proficient sight-reader gets his teeth into the thing, and experiences, probably for the first time in his life, the thrill of taking the music right off the page without too many disturbing errors. Everyone in the ensemble must get some sense of mastery over the notation; otherwise the sight-reading exercise is demoralizing. This is why it is so important to start with very simple music at a very slow tempo.

As a rule, vocalists read with some difficulty, so there is little chance that the section leaders, or anyone else in the choir, will get bored with the sight-reading material. In the band or orchestra, though, the virtuoso principals may read quite well. A secondary job then is to find something for these gifted youngsters to do while their friends learn how to sight-read. First of all, pass the conducting chores around. Concertmaster one day, first clarinetist next day, and so on, for the three- or four-minute sight-reading drill. Second, ask the principals in the orchestra to exchange instruments—concertmaster stepping over to play cello, principal cellist stepping over to play viola, and so forth. If the youngsters own rather expensive instruments and do not want to let just anyone play their instrument, let the violinist play a cello part an octave above or more. Give the first clarinet part to the first oboe, and the reverse; first flute part to first clarinet, and the reverse. In the band, give the first trombone part to the first tenor saxophone, and the reverse; the alto saxophone part to bass clarinet; E-flat clarinet to piccolo; and so on. Instruct all who are transposing to jump octaves when the notation goes above or below their instrument, or ask them to improvise in the proper style until the notation returns to their instrument.

Be not concerned at all with the horrendous musical results of these unorthodox procedures. It is a drill, remember, not a musical experience that occurs here. The object is to build sight-reading muscles in the rank and file of the ensemble, and to throw a challenge to the superstar principals. Transposition, improvisation, and doubling on several instruments are nearly lost skills in Western art music. The time and energy of the gifted principals will be profitably consumed thus, while their less talented associates struggle along with the rudiments of musical literacy.

Closing with a Familiar Work

Rehearsals tax the energy and patience of all who are involved. The end of a really productive rehearsal is likely to leave the students in a state of emotional and physical fatigue. A director should therefore time his work so that he has a few moments to perform a familiar composition to close the day's labor. The purpose is clear: to send the students out of the room with a sense of accomplishment and an attitude of enthusiastic anticipation of the next rehearsal.

EXPOSURE TO THE LITERATURE OF THE MEDIUM

Insofar as possible, members of a large performing ensemble should be confronted with the full range of published literature for the medium. Rather than polishing a few selections needed for concert programs, the teacher introduces the ensemble to many selections of varied type. Some of these are rehearsed carefully for concert use; others are read through or studied briefly so that they can become part of the pupils' background. This may prevent the group from doing certain especially difficult works in concert due to the necessity for limiting the time devoted to any one selection, but it may also result in better concerts as well as freeing rehearsal time for the survey of other worthy literature. The selections not destined for concert use may be examined with double purpose, for practice in reading and for acquaintance with literature, for example, or simply for the pleasure of becoming familiar with new and interesting music. Instead of spending the several months prior to a concert working intensely with the same repertoire, the youngsters meet one or two new selections at each rehearsal, review several that were introduced during earlier meetings, and look forward to enjoyable performing that includes but is not exclusively devoted to achieving perfection of the concert repertoire.

Learning about the history of music is a natural counterpart to the survey of music literature. Pupils who study music from the various eras of music history can develop a much clearer understanding of the progress of musical development than pupils who learn about it through study in the music history class. The experience of participating in the music and responding to its intellectual and emotional content leaves an impression no amount of reading can duplicate. The music director who takes rehearsal opportunities for exploring the literature of the medium is simultaneously taking an important step toward the teaching of music history. What remains is the task of giving direction to the experience by identifying and emphasizing the ideas to be learned.

Direct exploration results when the teacher plans concert and rehearsal programs to include works from the various periods of music history. In the course of a school year, some thirty-five weeks of from two to five rehearsal hours each week, there is opportunity for the director to present music from every significant period by every significant composer. This should be his aim. To define this learning more clearly, the teacher need give up only small portions of rehearsal time to discussion of the literature and its historical importance.

A few words about the formal design of the composition, or a few remarks on general stylistic traits, will suffice as a beginning. The musical style may be shown by performing and discussing a few selected measures from the music being rehearsed and from related music. Written assignments, quizzes, and other academic procedures may be needed to get best results here. There is no reason at all why members of performing ensembles cannot be expected to do a little academic work now and then for the general improvement of the entire music program. Credit toward graduation is granted quite universally these days; a modest academic responsibility will not endanger the popularity of the performing groups in the least.

SEATING ARRANGEMENTS: CHORAL GROUPS

There are many reasons for examining the various ways in which any chorus or glee club can be assigned to seats in the rehearsal room or standing positions on the concert stage. In arranging and rearranging the seating plan the teacher seeks to improve the musical effect and to adjust other factors as well. Where musical effect is concerned, the teacher strives to improve balance, intonation, and blend and to achieve ensemble and homogeneity of tone. He tries to provide support for the weaker parts and to place important parts next to each other to improve ensemble in special passages. The reasons other than musical have to do with the visual effect created by the placement of the group on the stage, the control and discipline of a large group of high-spirited pupils, and not unimportant, the ease and speed of checking attendance at rehearsals.

Balance can be improved by placing weaker voice groups where they can be heard and stronger ones where their tone is absorbed or covered. The weaker voice group is normally moved to the front so that its tone carries to the audience without having to penetrate the others. On some stages the weaker voice groups carry better if moved to the side or rear against a reflecting surface or if placed in an area of the stage that is acoustically live. Stronger voices are often placed behind the weaker ones or at either side. If placed at the sides, the singers can be turned to face the center of the stage, their voices being directed toward the conductor and the other singers rather than toward the audience. To reduce further the power of the stronger voices, they can be placed against and under stage draperies that absorb some of the tone.

Intonation can sometimes be improved by moving the offending part closer to the piano or another part that offers harmonic support. Sopranos, for example, may find it easier to sing in tune if they are placed close to basses who sing the foundation of the harmonic structure. Blend, closely related to intonation, can sometimes be improved by experimenting with the seating plan, moving certain parts closer to the piano or placing out-of-tune parts adjacent to those likely to be in tune. One source of difficulty is the common practice of placing boys behind the girls. Voices of adolescent boys tend to be heavy and guttural, especially basses whose natural desire is to sound like mature basses and who force their voices to achieve this effect. Placing these boys at the rear of the stage may cause them to force their voices even further and makes it difficult for them to hear the piano and the other parts. If they do sink below the pitch, they then pull the rest of the parts with them. The seating arrangement suggested in Figure 1 will help the boys stay on pitch.

The singing group achieves ensemble when it develops unanimity of feeling for attacks, releases, rhythms, dynamics, and the contours of phrases. To some extent this depends upon alert response to the conductor's signals, but it depends also upon each singer's musicianship and his intuitive feeling for the reactions of the other singers. Ensemble can be improved by revising the seating plan, moving certain singers or parts closer to the conductor or the piano, or by placing singers otherwise slow to respond between those who can lead them and provide assurance. Homogeneous tone can be achieved in the same way, voices of distinctive quality being placed among other voices to create a well-mixed choral tone in which no one voice is distinguishable in the mass. Weaker singers chronically uncertain of their parts or likely to deviate from the correct pitch can be surrounded by stronger singers. Finally, parts that often sing together can be placed next to each other so that each part can hear and follow the other in the passages they sing together.

Appearance is one of the nonmusical reasons for examining various seating possibilities. Rectangular, semicircular, and wedged-shaped groupings are desirable on some stages, whereas larger stages may suggest that the director place the chorus informally in several separate groups if the music and the skill of the chorus permit. In any case the

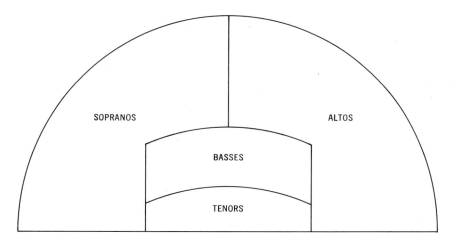

Figure 1 Chorus seating arrangement with male voices centered.

object is to please the eye and to relieve the monotony of static grouping. In rehearsal, an established seating plan aids the director in maintaining control over a large group. The very existence of a seating plan in which each singer is assigned to a permanent seat gives an impression of stability and order and acts as a deterrent when adolescent singers are tempted to indulge their volatile spirits. The teacher can take advantage of the seating plan to separate pupils who disturb the work of the group when seated together. An established seating plan speeds the chore of checking attendance, whether it is done by the teacher or by a student assistant. To this end the teacher keeps a seating chart always at hand, and the student assistant should have access to one when recording absences. A duplicate chart posted in the rehearsal room permits singers to find their seats quickly until they become accustomed to sitting in their assigned places.

The almost universally popular seating plan is the rectangle or semicircle in which all voices singing one part are grouped together. Groups are placed in front or rear, right or left depending upon the strength and ability of the singers who make up each part and upon the acoustical characteristics of the rehearsal room or concert hall. No choral director is content to follow an arrangement favored by another director working with a different chorus under different acoustical conditions. The final authority is always the ear of the director. It judges the effect created by the voices in his chorus singing the music he has selected in the concert hall in which his chorus must perform.

The relatively standard seating plan consisting of four groups of singers placed to form a rectangle can be varied to produce many different seating plans simply by changing the relative positions of the four groups within the rectangle. The chorus that has developed reading ability and vocal assurance can be grouped in quartets. This makes it almost impossible for the conductor to give cues to single parts, but results in superior blend and balance. The members of each quartet stand beside each other or can be arranged so that sopranos are in the front row of the chorus, altos in the second row, tenors in the third, and basses in the fourth. The teacher might find it interesting to experiment also with a heterogeneous seating plan, provided the singers are thoroughly familiar with their parts and can sing them independently with assurance. To achieve the heterogeneous mixture, the singers simply assemble informally without regard for part groupings in much the same way a congregation assembles in the pews of a church. Although this seems to conflict with all the rules of choral singing, the singers learn something from the experience. The director, if his chorus has been well trained, may be agreeably surprised by the tonal result.

Another possibility has to do with increasing the distance between singers. Many choral singers feel it is necessary to stand close to a neighbor so that the chorus becomes a tightly packed mass, assuming that proximity to other singers makes it easier to achieve unity of response. This is often true, but here again the director may experiment by asking the chorus to expand in width and depth until singers are four, six, or even ten feet apart. This forces the singers to be independent and at the same time requires that they listen intently for the other voices, and both of these results are desirable.

A seating plan, therefore, is more than a formula to be followed rigidly. There are almost limitless possibilities for varying the plan and for achieving special effects through rearranging the singers. There are general principles to be considered, but the principles need not be followed inflexibly. Each choral director grasps the opportunity to discover the seating plan best suited to his chorus. In doing so the director resists the tendency to accept stereotyped solutions and searches for originality because it may point the way to improved musical effect. A seating plan is another means for achieving satisfying musical results and is judged by the quality of the music it produces.

SEATING ARRANGEMENTS: INSTRUMENTAL GROUPS

Band Seating

Seating arrangements for the band are as flexible as its instrumentation. Here, again, there is much experimenting to improve balance and tone quality, and the director is free to seek the solution most appropriate for the characteristics of his situation. These characteristics include the total number of players, the number of each type of instrument, the relative size of sections, and the size, shape, and acoustics of the rehearsal room and concert hall. Figures 2 and 3 are two possible seating plans. The basic difference between them is in the placement of clarinets, normally the largest single section of the band. Many directors feel the clarinets are best placed in one large section as in Figure 2. Other directors have experimented by dividing the clarinets and placing all woodwinds close to the audience as in Figure 3.

In any arrangement there are almost limitless possibilities for variation. One rarely used plan seats all players in straight rows facing the audience, the conductor moving away from the band to be seen from each stand. The more common seating plans are based on semicircular

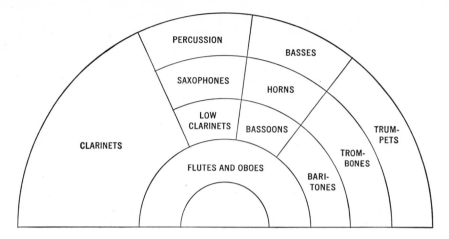

Figure 2 Band seating arrangement with clarinets together.

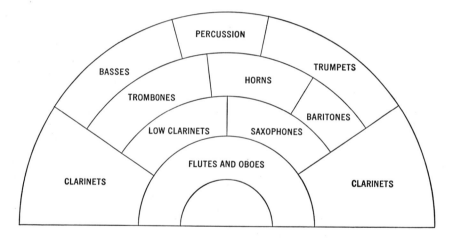

Figure 3 Band seating arrangement with clarinets divided.

rows with the conductor close to or at the center of the first semicircle. Many variations are possible even in this semicircular arrangement, but the principles to be considered when determining any seating plan are as follows:

1. Instruments with subdued tone are usually placed toward the front to permit their parts to carry to the audience.
2. Instruments with piercing tone are usually placed toward the rear, behind the screen of tone produced by other instruments.

3. Inner parts are sectioned together to improve their blend and facilitate ensemble playing.

4. Each section is grouped together, including the brass and woodwind sections in total and the subsections within each.

5. Flutes and oboes are usually placed well forward so that they can be heard and because of the frequency of solo passages in their parts.

6. Basses and percussion are usually placed in the last row, often in the center of the row, to be clearly audible to the rest of the band.

7. Horns are often placed directly in front of tubas, a practice desirable if programmed marches depend on the rhythmic interaction of their parts.

8. Trombones are often placed in the last row because this permits wide spacing and adequate slide room.

9. Baritones are placed where their frequent solo parts can be heard clearly by the audience.

10. Trumpets are placed in the last row because of their piercing tone, often toward the side of the stage so that bells point across stage instead of toward the audience.

Band players are accustomed to being assigned to seats for regular use during rehearsals and performance. There is merit in this practice in that it tends to eliminate confusion and helps pupils ready themselves for playing at the beginning of the rehearsal period. A standard procedure is to place players in order of ability—the best player in the first chair, the next best player in the second chair, and so on. Another possibility is to seat the best players where they can be of most help to pupils of less ability. One such plan is to place advanced players in outside positions on each stand, pairing each with a player of less skill. Another practical plan is to place best players in first chairs in each section—the best player on first stand, first part, the next best player on first stand, second part, the third best player on first stand, third part. This assures that each part will be played equally well and that balance will be even.

Orchestra Seating

The seating arrangement of the orchestra has been generally established during the years of its growth. There is less variation than in the seating arrangements for the band because of the relative newness of the concert band and the continuing experiments to improve its concert effect. The chief differences in orchestra seating are those resulting from differences in size and instrumentation. The small orchestra playing Baroque and early Classic music may use a seating plan different from that of the large orchestra playing late Romantic and Modern music.

The addition of large numbers of winds and percussion, and the distribution of solo passages among relatively unusual instruments, sometimes requires a revision of the seating plan.

Figures 4 and 5 are diagrams of two possible seating arrangements. The principal difference between them is in the placement of violins, the heart of orchestral tone. Figure 4 shows what is perhaps the most popular arrangement with all violins to the conductor's left. Figure 5 shows an arrangement which places first violins to the conductor's left and second

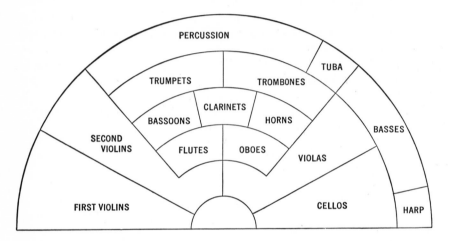

Figure 4   Seating arrangement for orchestra with violins together.

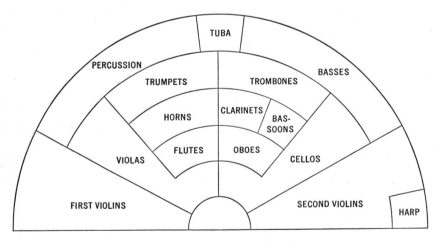

Figure 5   Seating arrangement for orchestra with violins divided.

violins to his right. Possibilities for variation of these seating arrangements are many, and it is to the conductor's advantage to experiment
with different arrangements to discover which is best for his orchestra.

The factors to be considered in planning the seating arrangement
are as follows:

1. Violin sections are seated together and placed where they can be
   heard by the audience. Because the instrument rests on the violinist's
   left shoulder with f-holes pointed toward his right, violins are most
   frequently seated to the conductor's left so that f-holes, rather than
   the backs of the instruments, face the audience.

2. Violas are sometimes given seating preference because they are usually
   few in number but must be heard. They might best be placed to the
   conductor's left if that position were not occupied by first violins. As
   an alternative, violas are often placed next to the first violins to the
   conductor's left, as in Figure 5, or next to the cellos and almost in front
   of the conductor, as in Figure 4.

3. Cellos are less of a problem than the other strings because their playing position tends to direct the tone forward. They are usually seated
   to the conductor's right, chiefly because other locations to his left are
   occupied by other strings.

4. Basses, like violins and violas, are somewhat "directional" in tone.
   They are normally played in a position that directs the tone to the
   player's right. For this reason they too might be best placed to the
   conductor's left so that f-holes face the audience. Because they frequently play passages in octaves with cellos, however, basses are usually placed in the last row near the cello section.

5. Flutes, oboes, clarinets, and bassoons are seated well forward near the
   middle of the orchestral semicircle. This permits their tone to carry to
   the audience and places them together to facilitate playing of ensemble
   passages.

6. Horns are seated near both woodwinds and brasses but as far forward
   as the seating plan permits. Their tone then carries to the audience,
   and they can join either woodwinds or brasses in ensemble passages.

7. Trumpets, trombones, and tuba are placed toward the rear and
   grouped together as a section with the tuba close to both percussion
   and basses.

It is especially important in the orchestra that better players be distributed throughout the sections instead of being concentrated at the
first several stands. There are often wide differences of ability among
the string players, and many of the less advanced players need help with
bowings, fingerings, and positions. For this reason it is desirable to place
violinists in this order:

Player 1: Violin I, first stand, first chair.
Player 2: Violin II, first stand, first chair.
Player 3: Violin I, second stand, first chair.
Player 4: Violin II, second stand, first chair.

In this arrangement, better players occupy first-chair positions at each stand, and less able players occupy second-chair positions at each stand. A good player is paired with a weaker player at each stand. First and second violins are well matched in both tone and technical facility. Bowings will be more nearly uniform. When pages are turned, usually by the second-chair player at each stand, the strings retain much of their tone. If better players are concentrated at the first several stands, string tone may drop as much as 75 percent at each page turn because half of the better players must stop playing to turn the page and many of the less able players at rear stands become confused or lose their places. In addition to following these general principles, the conductor who knows his players can pair pupils at stands for instructional, psychological, social, or other reasons and may find that minor changes in seating order result in major improvements in the playing of the orchestra.

Two final recommendations for rehearsal procedures are to begin and close each rehearsal on time, and to be positive and polite at all times. Begin and close on time means just that. No strolling in after the appointed hour. No begging for a few minutes more to clean up a difficult passage. The students are busy, and they should be dismissed on schedule. If extra, out-of-school rehearsals will be needed to prepare an important concert, the music teacher should give three or four weeks notice in advance. In many cases these special rehearsals demand that parents and neighbors get together to provide transportation and proper protection for their youngsters to and from the rehearsals. The director must take these pertinent factors into consideration.

Be positive and polite. "A little shorter on the eighth notes, please," is more instructional than, "Those eighth notes are still too long." Tell the youngsters what is wanted, not what is not wanted. And tell them in a straightforward manner without belittling them, or barking at them, or abusing them in any way. Negative tactics are sometimes effective, and, in certain situations, the teacher may have to start out with ruthless, dictatorial measures to get control of an especially unruly group. But under normal circumstances a positive, friendly, firm, courteous rehearsal manner will do the job quite nicely.

CHAPTER 7

Conducting Techniques

A music educator will save himself a world of time and labor if he learns to conduct his groups with forthright clarity and convincing authority. To do so he will have to work seriously at the job of becoming a conductor. Whatever he may have picked up in his college conducting course will be just enough to get him started on the right path. The real job begins with his first rehearsal of his own performing group at his first high school assignment. It is the intent of this chapter to reestablish certain principles of basic conducting, and to offer a few suggestions for the rather difficult task of self-instruction "on the job," as it were.

For purposes of discussion, two areas of conducting technique might be considered: (1) technique of the body—the manual actions which go into the art of conducting, and (2) technique of the mind—the mental processes which precede and coexist with the physical actions.

MANUAL TECHNIQUE

Carriage

A conductor should avoid all excesses which will detract from the job at hand. A brisk but not officious walk to the podium, a warm smile and the traditional bow to the audience, a relaxed but authoritative turn to the ensemble, and the concert is ready to begin. No stilted or affected mannerism, no extremes in personal grooming or clothing styles, no distractions. Avoid stooping, avoid leaning over or back to pull the music out of a section, avoid grotesque postures and gestures. Do not confuse flamboyance with emotional depth. The job is to conduct, not to dance or to act.

Right-hand Tradition

The right hand outlines the beat patterns, gives some cues, and describes, by the size and character of its pattern, the musical style wanted. The left hand comes into play for dynamics, many cues, phrasing nuances, balancing and blending, and all other needs. If used constantly to mirror the right hand's movements, the left hand loses its force. If allowed to rest at the conductor's side when not needed, then brought into play on special occasions, the left hand becomes an exceptionally dramatic tool for the conductor.

Right-hand conducting is most common. Left-hand conducting is rare. Left-handed people apparently take the traditional approach here out of deference to their musicians. The meter patterns would be reversed, and this would be likely to cause some trouble somewhere along the way for musicians long accustomed to the normal beat patterns.

The Baton

The baton serves as an extension of the right forearm, bringing greater dimension and clarity to the beat pattern. The wrist should be flexible, however, so that the baton may angle from the forearm for special expressive gestures now and then. Hold the baton between the ball of the thumb and the side of the index finger, palm down, hand cupped loosely around the heavy end of the stick.

A baton is frequently used with instrumental groups whenever there are ten to twelve or more performers. Use of the baton with choral groups is becoming more rare these days. There are no "proper" rules in these matters. Each conductor seems to be a law unto himself, and whatever objections his performers and audiences first have to his preferences are soon forgotten if he does his job well.

Basic Meter Patterns

Certain preconceived patterns are carved in the air for the basic meters. The general rule is that count ① goes down, the next most significant subsidiary count goes to the right, and the count just preced-

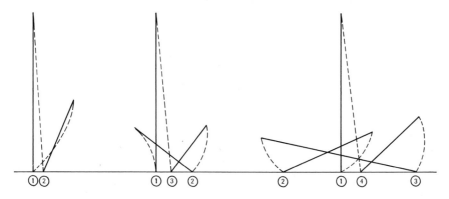

Figure 6 Conducting patterns for two-part, three-part, and four-part meters.

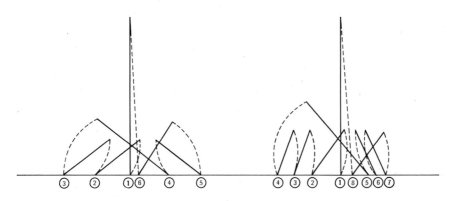

Figure 7 Conducting patterns for six-part and eight-part meters.

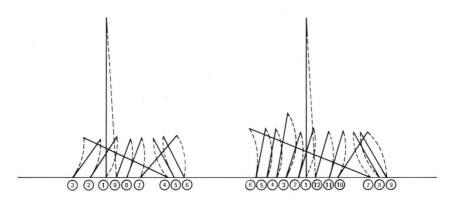

Figure 8 Conducting patterns for nine-part and twelve-part meters.

ing count ① goes up. From the general rule, and from traditional practice, the meter patterns shown in Figure 6 have come into common use. Full six-part, eight-part, nine-part, and twelve-part patterns follow similar principles (Figures 7 and 8).

Compressed six-part, nine-part, and twelve-part meters fall into the basic two-part, three-part, and four-part patterns, respectively. Compressed eight-part meters may fall into a two-part or a four-part pattern, depending upon style, tempo, and, to some extent, the conductor's personal taste.

Irregular Meter Patterns

A five-part, seven-part, ten-part, or any-part meter will usually lie in discernible units. The units may change from one measure to the next, but each measure on its own will usually have fairly easily identifiable unit sets. A measure of seven, for example, may be a unit of three followed by a unit of four, or the reverse. The conductor must determine the logical distribution of units, and conduct accordingly. Figure 9 shows two possibilities for any given measure of seven.

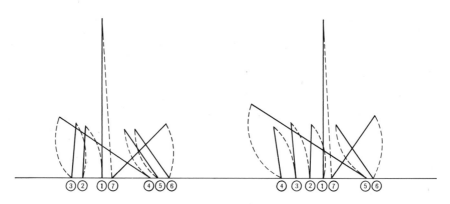

Figure 9 Two options for a measure in a seven-part meter.

Subdivisions

Subdividing meter patterns is merely a means of bringing greater control to smaller portions of the whole operation. As a general rule, the conductor simply beats twice or thrice in the framework of a normal pattern. A subdivided four would be, for example, down-down, left-left, right-right, up-up. The effect is not the same as a measure of eight. The conductor must choose the pattern which most effectively elicits the desired performance style from the musicians.

Ictus

In any beat pattern the exact instant of each separate beat should somehow be made perfectly clear to the performers. This exact instant is known as the ictus of the beat. The ictus need be nothing melodramatic, but it must be evident in each beat pattern. It consists of a feeling, as much as a visible gesture, in the mind of the conductor. For the performer it consists of something very subtle which the conductor does as the beat pattern unfolds. It may be a slight and fleeting bounce or tiny pulsation of the wrist at the exact instant of each separate beat; or it may be merely that the bottom-most point of each stroke occurs at precisely the instant of the metrical click in each pattern.

The ictus is the heart of the beat pattern. A beat pattern without an ictus for each stroke will lack definition, and there is a good chance that the group will have difficulty in precision performance. In even the most legato-style passages there must be an ictus, however modest and subtle, to each beat stroke in the pattern.

Stylistic Properties

In addition to the most evident and basic property of a beat pattern, the direction of its component strokes, there are at least three stylistic properties which greatly affect the way performers respond to the pattern: (1) weight, (2) resistance, and (3) the size, elevation, and advancement of the field of the beat pattern.

The weight of a beat pattern increases and decreases as greater or lesser amounts of the conductor's body are brought into the operation. In a given tempo and given dynamic level the stroke of a beat pattern might be executed with the wrist, with the forearm and wrist, with the forearm holding the wrist firm, or with the entire arm holding the wrist and elbow fairly firm. The weight of the beat pattern increases along the way, and the performers will respond differently in each situation.

Text, melodic structure, harmonic rhythm, and cadential patterns demand different kinds of conducting treatment, unrelated to dynamic level and the size of the performing group. "O Sacred Head Now Wounded," for example, seems to call for a beat pattern of considerable weight no matter how small or large the group or how loud or soft the overall sound.

The resistance within a beat pattern is most difficult to define. Description by example is easier. If a conductor were to execute his best pattern while standing on the floor of a swimming pool, the water would offer considerable resistance to the motion of his arm and baton. Contrast this kind of beat pattern with one in which the conductor stands, normally, in open air, and the idea is established. What is it that would make these two beat patterns different, assuming all other factors to be equal (size, tempo, etc.)? There would be a sense of greater muscular effort to produce the beat pattern under water. There would be hundreds of microscopic differences in the relative interworking of wrist, forearm, and upper arm. There would be a host of subtle changes in facial expression, in muscular tension around the neck and shoulders, and in the messages given and received by the eyes. There would be greater "resistance" in the entire character of the beat pattern. The result would be a different response from a group of performers. As a rule, the greater the resistance of the beat pattern, the greater will be the majesty and grandeur of the performer's response.

The size, elevation, and advancement of the field of the beat pattern elicit significantly different responses from performers in the same manner as weight and resistance. The size of a beat pattern depends upon the size of the group being conducted, to be sure, but it also depends upon the dynamic level wanted by the conductor, the tonal density required to support the dynamic level, and the general character of the phrasing needed to make the whole thing convincing. By simply changing the size of the beat pattern a conductor brings an entirely different demand to his performers.

A beat pattern also has a horizontal plane of reference known sometimes as the beat floor, or the tessitura of the beat pattern, or the beat table, or the elevation of the beating field. This is simply the level at which most significant movements occur in the conductor's beat gestures. This beat table is just a little above the elbow, in front of the body, for most conductors, and for good reason: it is the most natural, most comfortable, and least fatiguing level, and it allows for greatest freedom and coordination of movements of the upper arm, elbow, forearm, and wrist. Conductors sometimes adjust their beat table, subconsciously, perhaps, to compensate for their stature. Tall conductors sometimes develop a beat table that is too low for them; short conductors often raise their beat table to ensure that their performers can always see all conducting movements. For maximum freedom and most natural authority, a beat table just above the elbow level is recommended. Let the adjustments come in the relative heights of the conductor's stand and the podium.

The conducting field may be quite some distance from or very close to the body. This property, called advancement, does not affect the performer's response as much as the elevation or size of the beating field. It contributes greatly, though, to the conductor's overall manner and thus, directly to the response of even those performers who are not in a position to detect any great change in the advancement of the field. When the conductor pulls his conducting field close to his body, it is fairly certain that he wants the dynamic level lowered, or an increased transparency in the ensuing sonorities, or some kind of reduction in the musical offering. On the other hand, when the conductor advances his baton in the direction of the cellos, he most assuredly invites them to give their finest in the approaching passage. Indeed, if the musical statement is of great import, the conductor will even take a step in the direction of the heroes of the moment, advancing his conducting field to the limits of the podium area. This kind of strolling around the podium is not recommended. Suffice to turn to the performers charged with the musical responsibility of the moment, to advance the conducting field a bit in their direction, and to trust that they will respond in adequate measure.

Entrances

The term *attack* has been deliberately avoided here. *Entrance* does the job quite nicely, and does away with the suggestion of explosive energy.

The general rule for all entrances is simply this: give a small preparatory beat, in the style and in the tempo of the music to come, then bring in the ensemble on the next full beat. In 4/4 meter thus, to bring an ensemble on count ①, the conductor gives a small preparatory beat (which really functions, in his mind and in the minds of the performers, as an imaginary, "free" count ④), then comes straight down, in tempo, for count ①. In 4/4 meter, to bring an ensemble in on count ④, the conductor gives a small preparatory beat (a "free" beat ③, really), then delivers the normal beat ④ on which the ensemble enters. The preparatory beat, in all cases, must not be too generous lest someone mistake it for the real entering stroke.

For anacruses, "pick-up notes," the conductor beats, as his preparatory beat, the last fundamental count previous to the count on which the anacruses occur, then beats the full count on which the anacruses occur. The ensemble enters at the appropriate instant within this full count. Even among the professionals this is tricky business, and is always worked out very carefully in rehearsal. Public school directors must work these matters out very carefully, for adolescents will simply not enter unless they are fairly confident they should.

Releases

The release, or "cutoff," signals the performers to cease producing sound. At the end of a long decrescendo to *pianississimo* the release may be nothing more than gathering the arms low and in front, and fading out. In more vigorous situations the release may be a brilliant and dramatic spasm of the wrist and forearm. Whatever its character, the release is relatively quick, circular, and executed with wrist and forearm. The circular motion may be either clockwise or counterclockwise. The entire release gesture should always be in keeping with the musical situation.

The size and direction of the release should be so ordered as to facilitate the conductor's next task, be it to introduce a new phrase, or to hold the audience in silence while the ensemble gets ready for the next movement in the music, or to step off the podium to take a bow.

Choral conductors sometimes develop a technique of quickly closing thumb and forefinger on one or both hands to signal the cessation of a vowel sound or to signal the closing of a vowel sound to a resonant consonant sound. This may soon grow to be a rather affected mannerism, and it is not recommended.

Cues

Cues are signals to performers to join in the musical offering. A cue may be given with either hand, with the eyes, or with a nod of the head. The purpose is always the same: to prepare the performers for their entrance and to prepare the audience for what might otherwise be an unexpected shock.

To bring a performer in, to "cue him in," a conductor should turn his eyes to the direction of the performer, catching his eye for a moment before the entrance is to occur. A few beats before the entrance, the left hand comes up and is sustained without undue motion until the beat-before-entry arrives. At this beat-before-entry the left hand drops slightly in the manner of a preparatory beat. Then, on the beat-of-entry itself, the firm cue is given.

Fermatas

A fermata may be nothing more than a phrase indication, or it may be a full stop in the musical activities, or any gradation in-between. It always calls for careful examination to ensure that everyone knows exactly what to expect and what to do.

Generally, the beat pattern leading into the fermata causes no difficulty. The difficulty arises in trying to get out of the thing with some grace and poise. Two conditions exist: the fermata which terminates in a complete stop, and the fermata which leads directly into more music. In the fermata with full stop, a complete release is executed, and a separate preparatory beat given for the ensuing music. Each stroke is a separate item. In the fermata without full stop the release of the fermata is at once also the preparatory beat for the ensuing music. One stroke serves both needs.

MENTAL TECHNIQUE

Score-Reading

Young music directors are frequently intimidated by the complexities of a full score. They should be. The full score requires hours of careful study before it is of any functional utility to the director. It is so far superior to first violin or first cornet parts, to piano reductions, and to abbreviated scores, however, that the young music director should start right out using a full score for everything he rehearses and conducts. In a very short time, then, he will feel at ease with a full score in front of him even if he has some distance to go before the score really comes alive for him.

The textbooks say that a conductor should be able to sit at the piano, score in hand, and take the music off the page, and he should be able to sit at his desk, score in hand, and hear everything in his mind's ear. Nonsense. There are thousands upon thousands of fine conductors of professional, civic, public school, college, and miscellaneous orchestras, bands, and choirs who cannot play piano enough to help themselves very far along in score-reading and who could not come very close to anything like hearing a complex score while sitting at their desk. Score-reading is not an exercise in transportation and keyboard prowess; nor is it an exercise in transposition and sight-singing facility.

Score-reading is the art of extracting from the printed page the sequence of essential musical gestures as they will be delivered by the machinery of the medium. The conductor creates for himself a line which contains the significant musical events, complete with qualifying expressive adjustments, as these events will be presented by the voices or instruments. It is not essential that the conductor be able to produce every last musical gesture at its proper pitch at the piano or in his mind. Indeed, in many modern scores the piano is of absolutely no use whatsoever, for the musical gestures may not have traditional pitches and qualities.

It is essential that a conductor be able to determine which is most significant of the many musical events going on at any one time, how much attention should be given to concomitant details elsewhere, how elaborate the expressive interpretation should be, what should be the relative weight and prominence of the various components, and other such questions of musical judgment.

How does a new music director go about training himself to work with full scores? He starts while still in school. He starts by purchasing the full score to the works he is currently performing with his college ensemble. While the college orchestra director works his way through a rehearsal, the director-to-be follows all that transpires in his own score, marking things here and there that will be of value later. Upon his graduation from music school, then, a new music director has a repertoire of compositions the full scores to which he knows really quite well. Many of these compositions will be too difficult for high school groups; many will also be quite within high school technical capacities. In either case the director has learned much about full scores.

The new director should also start a program of purchasing full scores to works he is likely to conduct in the future, even though he may not perform them during his college career. His college ensemble director could give him a list of at least a dozen compositions he will probably conduct before his career gets along too far. The aspiring director should purchase these scores and begin his professional conductor's library while still in school.

With his library of scores growing year by year, the ensemble director-to-be then takes every opportunity to conduct the compositions from full score, vicariously, with college ensembles, with high school groups in the area, with records and tapes. In his mind he pictures himself on the podium, conducting the work with confidence and assuredness. Little by little he gets a feeling for what is and what is not crucial in these full scores, and he makes tentative judgments on cues, releases, and the rest of the gestures of the trade. Before long he will have built up a fairly substantial body of musical information and technical ideas which augur well for his future career.

Explanations and Corrections

In spite of his most careful physical motions, a conductor will have to stop his ensemble to explain and correct things now and then. The explanations should be relevant to the passage of music under hand, should not wander into distant areas, and should be expressed in a vocabulary and in terminology which the young musicians understand. A music director who stops his ensemble to explain something about the Classic Period may or may not be consuming rehearsal time effectively. The information should bear directly on the musical problem of the moment, and the students must see this connection clearly. If they do not, they will politely listen to the information then proceed to play exactly as they had before.

Corrections should be precise, impersonal, entirely clear, and within the technical proficiencies of the young musicians. Correction by negative example always runs the danger of offending the youngsters. Correction by positive example sometimes fails to make the point. Correction by exaggerated positive example works well with adolescents.

Tempo

Aside from the physical, manual technique of indicating the velocity of the metrical pulses, the whole concept of tempo will cause a new director no end of concern. When an ensemble enters at a tempo slower than he had intended, for example, what should the conductor do? String along with them, unhappy all the way through the entire composition? Bring them into line instantly with the correct tempo, no matter how odd it will sound to the audience? Pull them up gradually? Carry on, and by internal adjustments, try to make the slower tempo convincing? As a rule, it is probably best to bring the whole thing instantly into line, however odd the audience might think it happened to be. Better to have the audience say, "They got off to a bad start, but things seemed to clear up soon," than to have them say, "What was wrong with that second number? I was uncomfortable—and so was the conductor, apparently—through the whole twelve minutes."

Some conductors seem to have nearly continual trouble with their ensemble's dragging behind them a good share of the time. These conductors usually create their own problem by unconsciously calling for the very thing they want most desperately to correct. When the group begins to lag, the conductor immediately increases the size of his beat pattern, increasing at the same time, usually, the weight and resistance of the beat pattern. He then frowns and looks around for offending performers while he pumps away furiously at almost the exact speed as had been in effect. He continues to labor, keeping his ictus very close to the metronomic velocity of the ensemble's performance. He feels, erroneously, that if he puts his ictus too far ahead of his performers the entire performance will disintegrate. He feels that he must stay with the group.

He should, rather, reduce the size of the beat pattern; increase the clarity, precision, and snap of the ictus; frown at any and all who glance up his way; put the ictus exactly where he wants it; and wait until they catch up and solidify things. They will. It may take a few measures, but if they are with him at all, they will fall into the new, proper tempo before too many measures go by.

Because of their limited technical proficiency, public school groups have more than their share of tempo problems. The conductor should establish his tempos very clearly at all times, and insist that the youngsters come along, however insecure they may feel about the whole thing.

Tempo accelerando and ritardando need a word or two. Performers should have a little time to prepare for the change coming up and to reestablish themselves after the change has run its course. It is recommended, therefore, that just before a ritardando, the beat size be increased a little to accommodate the slower tempo coming up, and just as the tempo is about to return to its former state, the beat size be reduced a little to forecast, as it were, the change to come. In accelerando the beat size should be reduced just before, and increased just coming out of the change. These accommodations in the size of the beat pattern help to offset the performer's inclination to be late with his change and to go too far with the change.

Soloists, Accompanists, Combined Forces

The larger the group, the greater the need for catering to its needs. If a soprano soloist enters too early, for example, it is much more reasonable to try to cue her out or suspend her for a moment than to try to get sixty to seventy-five other singers to jump three measures ahead for her. Likewise with small groups pitted against large groups. The large group must be given first consideration in the case of crossed signals or inaccurate cuing.

Accompanists always suffer at the every impulse of the conductor. They must learn this during their first few hours as accompanists. If they cannot adjust, they will be unhappy nearly all of the time, and it is best to replace them with those who can tolerate such working conditions.

Professional Personality

A conductor's private personality is his own business. He may be lovable, kind, and modest; or he may be unlovable, cruel, and a braggart. In the long-range view of things this private personality will affect his career only to the extent that he mingles with those people who are in a position to cause some change in his professional career.

A conductor's professional personality, though, is a different matter, and it bears heavily on how his ensemble performs. From a professional standpoint the following traits seem to be common among the better conductors: (1) they are self-righteous and authoritarian, (2) they are orderly and predictable, and (3) they are decisive and persuasive.

Self-righteousness and authoritarianism are ordinarily considered undesirable attributes. Perhaps they are. Certain people, though, need a bedrock faith in their own conscience and in their instinctive beliefs. Military leaders, corporation executives, poets—indeed, all who stand out from the crowd in one manner or another—need a touch of self-righteousness in their personality to carry them through periods of criticism and disfavor. Conductors certainly need it. The podium is no place for dialogue. Public performance is not for people who do not believe in what they are doing. The better conductors seem to be rather comfortably set in their ways.

Orderliness is considered a virtue. Predictable behavior may or may not be a virtue. The better conductors seem to have worked out systems for their professional activities which permit them to get a lot of work done in a short time. They are busy people, and order greatly reduces wasted time and energy. Order is based on predictability; hence, the two traits often go hand in hand.

A conductor's job is essentially a continual involvement in making decisions and in persuading others that the decisions are valid. New music directors should try to develop a habit of making decisions "on the spot." If a question in dynamics or tempo arises, decide then and there what will be done, and stick to the decision if it is reasonable to do so. Avoid the habit of saying, "Let me check that tonight; we will decide tomorrow."

Since they are accustomed to getting their way, conductors seem to build up a momentum of persuasion. On and off the podium they tend to dominate conversations, to make their influence felt in all manner of things, and to persuade others that their beliefs are worth serious consideration. A new music teacher must try to keep this kind of behavior in control, off the podium, but he should plunge headlong into the game, on the podium.

All in all, a conductor's task is frightfully complex. He must master the stick, he must learn to read full scores, he must practice making decisions. The hours are long, the pay is only fair, the social status is none too high. But the purpose is noble, the work exciting, and the inner rewards more than enough to compensate for other limitations. Most of all, the exhilaration of standing on the podium in front of fifty to sixty youngsters and leading them through a fine piece of music is a unique and truly satisfying experience. It behooves all music teachers-to-be to take great pains in preparing themselves for this privilege and responsibility.

CHAPTER 8

Performance Considerations

Performances by public school bands, choirs, and orchestras are a natural outcome of the school's enormous investment in the music program. The performances have musical, educational, and social values of great importance to the school and to the community. A new music teacher should have some idea of his prerogatives and responsibilities before he plunges into preparing concerts and shows.

PERFORMANCE GOALS

Because there are many reasons for presenting an ensemble in performance, and many possibilities for achieving desirable outcomes, the music teacher will do well to establish the goals he hopes to reach in his work. Among these goals, assuredly, are the musical growth of the young musicians entrusted to his care, and the development of good community relations.

Musical Growth

Performance can be a learning experience for the student musicians, helping them advance beyond the limits of progress possible through participation in rehearsals only. Performance provides motivation for rehearsal, offering incentive which spurs the group to concentrated effort.

Performance provides for the application of skill, requiring youngsters to be alert and to exercise their skills to perform well despite the pressures and tensions created by the presence of an audience; the difference between the atmosphere of rehearsal and that of performance impels pupils to concentrate all their powers and raise their efforts to a peak of perfection not common to the rehearsal.

There are further advantages in performance in that it tends to promote pupil development in areas not directly related to the performing skill. It is one means of raising the pupils' level of music taste. In the classroom or in the rehearsal, pupils respond best to music they enjoy, and the teacher is prone to seek this response by selecting materials to maintain interest rather than widen acquaintance with superior music. When preparing for a concert, however, pupils accept the necessity for studying music that has less immediate appeal for them. They are quick to see the desirability of offering music that appeals to the many different tastes among audiences and are willing to work hard to prepare music of high caliber, knowing that by doing so they win the approbation of those who listen. When the director applies this knowledge to the selection of materials for concert programs, he takes advantage of pupils' higher levels of interest to introduce them to superior music, persevering in its study until the group reaches a level of performing excellence that displays the beauties of the music.

One of the important performance goals is to develop the young musicians' poise and self-confidence, qualities which can be developed rapidly through the experience of appearing before an audience. Of further benefit to pupils is the fact that performance is enjoyable and stimulating in a general way. Pupils of all ages enjoy the experience of appearing in public, especially if they appear as members of a large group and are spared the stronger pressure of solo or small ensemble performance. This enjoyment is a physical and emotional outlet, worthy for itself as well as for the stimulation it provides for music study in rehearsal.

Community Relations

Performing music groups are among the most effective means of arousing community interest and support. The public concert is of especial interest because it is enjoyable; audiences gather to be entertained, and parents are gratified to see their children perform. When the concert offers a lesson to the audience through its implications concerning the general value of the educational program, the lesson being combined with entertainment and enjoyment, it makes a deeper impression than similar information presented through other public relations devices.

There is a more practical financial aspect to the public concert. In some instances admission can be charged to raise funds for special purposes. Money can be gathered to augment the choir robe fund, to expand the orchestra library, or to purchase special equipment necessary to the band program. The performing group can lend its assistance to other school departments, helping the dramatics group gather funds for scenery and costumes, helping clubs buy special materials or equipment, or participating in fund drives of benefit to the entire school.

Many educators feel it is improper for a music group to charge admission to its concerts. The school music program is a tax-supported educational activity, and its concerts should be open to the public and free. The director is a teacher of music whose function it is to guide the music development of pupils in his charge; it is not his responsibility to participate directly in the gathering of funds to support either the school or the music program. If he does so, especially if the funds obtained are used solely for the advancement of the music program, he may be trespassing in an area beyond the proper limits of professional endeavor. There is something unfair, too, about a practice that permits the music groups to exploit their entertainment value to serve their own ends when other and more basic subjects in the school program are unable to resort to similar measures.

Nevertheless, there are many school music organizations that raise funds through concerts. The practice may be justifiable when the performing group is new and growing, when it is obviously below the standard of similar groups in neighboring schools, and when the school budget is such that the allocation of regular funds must be postponed until later years. In these circumstances school administrators may agree to the necessity for raising funds through extraordinary means, and other teachers may endorse the project and even cooperate in carrying it out.

Because the public concert can be used effectively to secure extramusical benefits, the music teacher must be alert to the dangers of exploiting pupil abilities to achieve ends neither musical nor educational. There are serious dangers arising from the entertainment value of the concert. Because audiences respond favorably to entertaining concerts, and pupils are especially responsive to concert music they enjoy singing, the music director is often tempted to build concert programs with these ends in view. Entertainment, however, is not the principal goal of music education. Neither is it proper to use pupils to further the cause of music or to achieve objectives desired by the music director if this use exploits the group at the expense of educational progress. Proper goals are those that have to do with education in general and with the teaching of music in particular.

CONCERT OPPORTUNITIES

Because the performing experience is of educational value, it is appropriate that the music director seek opportunities for his pupils to appear in public. These opportunities are legion. There are school concerts of many different kinds and for many different groups as well as public concerts under the auspices of various community organizations. By scheduling concerts for different audiences, the teacher provides repeated performing experience without requiring the preparation of an extensive concert repertoire. This is advantageous in that the young musicians are not forced beyond the limits of their interest because of the pressures of a heavy performance schedule. Each concert selection can be prepared carefully and without sacrifice of the rehearsal time that should be devoted to other learning experiences. Once worthy selections have been thoroughly prepared, they can be performed on repeated occasions; it is neither desirable nor efficient to spend months in the rehearsal of concert music used only once before the group must begin the study of an entirely new program.

School Concerts

In the school itself the large ensemble can participate in regular assemblies, utilizing an entire assembly period for its concert or occupying only a short portion of a number of assembly periods. The latter procedure is desirable because the ensemble can present its performance after mastering only a few selections, permitting the teacher to offer this kind of motivation without waiting for the several months required to prepare music for a lengthy program. School songs, patriotic songs, and other appropriate music can be performed as a regular part of every assembly, or the group can be used to lead and accompany the singing of the entire student body. During holiday seasons or on other special occasions the ensemble can prepare a complete program in the form of an informal concert. This may be solely for the enjoyment of the student body, may prompt the invitation of parents to visit the school assembly, or may serve as a dress rehearsal for a public concert. On still other occasions the large performing groups can cooperate with a dramatics group or some other school club in presenting an assembly program of a special nature in which music plays a subordinate role.

Similar programs can be arranged for presentation in other schools of the community, the high school band, chorus, or orchestra offering programs in junior high and elementary schools. In addition to providing performance opportunities for the high school musicians, this practice stimulates interest in the high school music program itself, encouraging pupils in the junior high school to plan in advance for membership and reducing the problem of recruiting in the high school. The appearance of the high school performing ensemble in a junior high school assembly may have a desirable influence on the junior high school as well, encouraging membership and providing a model of good music for the junior high school music groups to imitate. A further possibility is that of exchange concerts with schools in neighboring communities to broaden pupils' experience and acquaint them with the work done by other schools. This cooperative arrangement is much to be desired and creates a far better atmosphere than the competitive spirit fostered by music contests, school sports, and other such activities.

An area worthy of exploration, especially for the small ensembles and soloists who may be a part of the larger organizations, is the music recital. In some schools extended lunch periods leave pupils with unoccupied time during the middle of the day. In others there are club, homeroom, and other activity periods that can be utilized for music. The hour immediately after school and in some cases a period of perhaps fifteen minutes before school might be made available for special musical purposes. These periods are ideally suited for the music recital, a brief, informal concert presented by soloists or small groups. Concerts of this nature may be open to anyone who wishes to attend, there being no necessity for requiring the attendance of the entire school or an entire class.

The experience of appearing in recital is a valuable one for young musicians. An audience of almost any size, from a few pupils to an entire class or the entire school, is suitable and provides the desired performing experience. Recitals encourage the performing pupils to gain independence, arranging their own rehearsals, planning recital dates and programs, and conducting the recital itself. It also permits the performers to explore types of music of special interest to them and to various segments of the student body. Music of a lighter nature is almost certain to be successful, and music representing a particular country or historical period may be of interest to special classes. Once interest is developed and the recital performers have gained skill and assurance, the recital program may be extended to include evening concerts in the school building or to presentations for various community groups.

Public Concerts

Opportunities for public concerts are equally numerous. Formal public concerts can be presented on a regular basis throughout the school year, appropriate programs being arranged during holiday seasons or for annual concerts in the spring or fall. The band, chorus, or orchestra can appear before PTA meetings or for other school functions to which the public is invited. Other concerts for interested community groups offer a means of supplementing the regular school concert programs. Churches of the community may welcome the high school glee club, for example, especially if it is possible to arrange a combined program shared by the glee club and the church choir. Service clubs and other community organizations present special programs in which high school instrumentalists can participate. The chorus can be of real service by presenting concerts in hospitals and other community institutions. In some communities, radio and television stations are willing to provide time for broadcast concerts, especially during holiday seasons. The broadcasting experience is an exciting one for the young musicians, creating strong interest and stimulating the improvement of their art. The teacher must exercise good judgment, however, in scheduling radio and television appearances, for imperfections of intonation and ensemble are magnified by the microphone.

Public concerts, including those on radio and television, are of value because they permit the music groups to appear before audiences composed of adults, creating a concert climate quite different from that of the school concert in which they perform for other pupils of their own age. The opportunities for public concerts, combined with those for concerts in the school or at school functions, are so numerous that the music teacher may find it necessary to select performance opportunities carefully to prevent the too-frequent performance that overtaxes his chorus. If good judgment is exercised in scheduling concerts, however, the experience is of great educational value to the youngsters.

THE CONCERT CALENDAR

Restrictions

The necessity for planning the concert calendar carefully is evident when the limitations of the young musicians in the high school or junior high school music groups are considered. They are neither physically nor vocally capable of an extended series of concerts. Because they are not trained musicians with highly developed skills, reading abilities, and music sensitivity, they must be given adequate time to master the concert repertoire. Rehearsal time is limited. Their interests and energies are divided among music activities, school studies, and many extracurricular projects. If the ensembles are to be a source of general music learning, rehearsal time must provide for surveying the literature and history of music, learning numerous music skills, and developing interest and appreciation. The music teacher cannot justifiably regard the group as an organization having performance as its sole objective. Moreover, the performing group should not be permitted to develop to the point at which it claims the major share of the pupils' attention or occupies too many of their hours either in or out of school. Other school subjects must take precedence in the curriculum and in the demands placed upon pupils' time. Thus it is important that the teacher restrict the performance schedule and plan it carefully so that it can be carried out effectively without making unreasonable demands on the pupils.

Scheduling

In planning the concert calendar the teacher begins by considering the concerts of a regular nature that occur on an annual basis, perhaps placing these on the calendar a year in advance. In doing so he considers the demands placed on pupils, the probability of extraordinary situations which might require pupils to be called out of classes for special rehearsals, the quantity and type of music needed to fill these concert programs, and the necessity for securing administrative approval for every concert and rehearsal not held during regularly scheduled hours.

It is especially important that the music teacher concern himself with the manner in which music activities interfere with or detract from other portions of the school program. The music teacher who constantly requests that pupils be excused from other classes for special rehearsals quickly generates antipathy among administrators and other teachers for the music program. Similarly, it is important that the school principal or superintendent be consulted about the advisability of scheduling public concerts that may conflict with other school or community activities. The music program needs the support of administrators and other teachers, and the fact that it is of natural interest to the public and receives much public attention may create resentment among teachers whose work must be confined to the classroom.

A faculty steering committee is sometimes appointed for this purpose. Such a committee might be composed of the music teacher, teachers from several other departments, including those with interests in athletics and dramatics as well as the core subjects, and the principal as an *ex officio* member. By discussing the concert calendar and other problems with this committee, the music teacher in effect seeks the advice and assistance of the entire faculty. He informs them of the problems involved in managing the music program, of providing the best educational experience for his young musicians, and ensures that planned concert activities have the full approval of the entire school. As a further safeguard the recommendations of this steering committee can be presented to the faculty during regular faculty meetings so that plans can be discussed and approved by the entire group when necessary.

In planning concert appearances the music teacher must be certain to consult the school calendar. In many school systems a master calendar is maintained in the office of the principal or superintendent. This calendar shows dates when school begins and ends for the year, vacation periods, and special holidays. It should also show the dates set aside for special events, including the administration of achievement and placement tests for the entire student body, the ends of marking periods, dates for completion of records and forms, periods for health examinations, inoculations, and so forth. Each of these might offer sufficient reason for postponing a music concert. In addition, this calendar should show dates selected for various extracurricular activities such as sports, dramatic productions, special school assemblies, and PTA meetings. The music teacher consults this calendar before selecting concert dates to avoid conflict with other school functions and to make certain all concert dates are entered on the master calendar for the information of groups planning other extracurricular activities.

Teacher-Pupil Planning

To free himself from some of the details of concert planning, and to encourage pupil participation, the music teacher designates a student group as a planning or program committee. It is the teacher's responsibility to plan aspects of the music program that require his experienced music judgment and to approve or revise the decisions of the committee, but much of the clerical and routine work can be carried out by competent pupils. This is a desirable application of principles of student government to the music program. The existence of a student committee increases interest in the performing activities of the group, stimulates pupil cooperation, and prevents some of the problems that arise when concert dates conflict with the students' other activities.

The latter problem is of consequence especially when the ensemble becomes capable of artistic performance and receives many concert invitations from community groups. If the concert calendar is planned by the students themselves, it is less likely that soloists and leaders of the various sections will have conflicting social engagements on the evenings of important concerts. The student committee reviews invitations from community groups and other sources, recommending their acceptance or rejection. The existence of the committee is valuable from the teacher's point of view because it relieves him of some of the necessity for explaining to community groups the reasons for refusing certain concert invitations. The concert calendar is arranged by a committee according to an organized and equitable system; thus, it is possible to avoid the implication that some community groups are given preferred treatment.

Keeping Records

Planning is made easier if records are maintained, permitting the director to refer to them for information concerning the events of previous years. By preserving concert calendars, the music director can at any time determine which concerts arise annually, which community groups submit concert invitations, the frequency with which invitations from any one group are accepted, and the general pattern of concert activities as it develops over a period of years. By establishing a file of printed programs from past concerts, he can determine which works have been performed, which have been presented to various community groups, and which have been studied in previous years by students who are still members of the group. By adding a few brief notes after every concert, he can record information concerning audience reaction, quality of performance, and the degree of pupil interest in each concert selection.

These notes are of inestimable value to the director as he plans subsequent programs. They permit him to select from the repertoire music appealing to audiences and students. The file of printed programs provides information on which to base a rotating schedule of music to be studied in rehearsal so that pupils who remain in the group for more than one year do not study the same music over and over again. By examining his files, the director projects the concert schedule for the coming year, including both the concerts that arise regularly and those likely to be needed for special occasions or in response to invitations from community groups. In addition, the files permit him to project rehearsal schedules for an entire year, indicating the number and kind of concert selections needed, the amount of rehearsal time to be devoted to them, and the amount of rehearsal time that may be reserved for other music study.

With this planning completed, the music director is able to post a concert schedule in the rehearsal room for the information of the pupils in the group, advising them of concert dates well in advance so their other activities may be planned accordingly. If he wishes, he can post rehearsal schedules several weeks in advance for the information of members and to guide the librarians who distribute music before it is to be rehearsed and remove it from the folders after it has been presented in concert. The files and other records then serve a useful purpose, guiding the work of the group, saving time for both director and students, and helping rehearsals and concerts proceed smoothly.

THE CONCERT PROGRAM

The preparation of concert programs has an influence on the judgment and taste of the students involved in the programs. The succession of rehearsals devoted to intensive study of good literature for band, chorus, or orchestra provides the extensive experience, the repeated contact, and the increased knowledge that strengthen pupil interest in and understanding of worthy music. Similarly, the concert is a means of acquainting audiences with better music, taking advantage of parents' natural interest in the achievements of their children to direct their attention toward great musical works that might otherwise be of little interest to them. Because the public concert is such a strong force, the music director must take great care to prepare each concert for maximum musical, social, and educational returns.

Unity, Variety, Contrast

In building each concert program the director strives to include both unity and variety in a presentation of reasonable length. It is necessary that audience interest be sustained and that the concert be brought to a conclusion before the listener becomes fatigued. A unified program provides a thread of continuity to lead the listener from one selection to the next, whereas variety and contrast combat the natural waning of interest as the program continues. Unity can be provided through the selection of a theme for each concert, or several themes that permit the grouping of selections into related units. Themes may be suggested by the season of the year, important holidays, or periods in music history. Holiday programs are usually successful because of the atmosphere generated by the holiday itself and because the appropriate music is often well known to and enjoyed by the audience. Programs devoted to a historical period or a particular type of music literature may arouse interest because of the presentation of unusual types of music. In addition, they give the music director an opportunity to extend his teaching to include the listeners as well as the performers. In doing so he builds acceptance of worthy literature unfamiliar to his audiences and paves the way to subsequent concerts of high caliber.

Variety and contrast may be achieved in a number of ways. Because the public school ensembles usually present concerts consisting of a number of short selections rather than lengthy compositions, it is possible to choose contrasting selections and to arrange the order of their presentation to provide changes in mood, tempo, and style.

The program may be varied further by the inclusion of soloists and small ensembles such as trios and quartets. This is desirable in that it provides a challenging outlet for the more talented members of the group and avoids the fatigue young musicians may experience when presenting a lengthy concert by themselves.

From sixty to ninety minutes is a reasonable maximum length for the concert program. This may vary, being influenced by the type of music presented, the abilities of the performers, and the interest of the audience, and being further adjusted by the inclusion of an intermission. Moreover, the director may find that a concert well received by one audience subsequently proves too long or too short for another. In any event, the music director may well follow the show business adage that it is better to do one song too few than one too many.

The usual audience of pupils or of parents who gather to see their children perform shows a limited capacity for listening and may become restless during an extended program. Thus it is advisable to plan the concert in such a way that audience fatigue is avoided and that even the last selection can be presented to interested and attentive listeners. Principal offenders in this respect are the departmental concerts in which an attempt is made to display to the public all the groups in the school music program. Concerts of this kind are sometimes planned for the end of the school year, music festivals which show the progress of the many pupils in the various groups. Although there may be a festival atmosphere about such a program and an air of excitement caused by the massing of large numbers of pupils, the audience sometimes sees little beyond the parade of one group after another before the footlights, an interminable process of little interest to parents whose children appear for only a few brief selections before being replaced by other pupils in other groups. Rather than permit a concert of this sort to grow beyond reasonable time limits, the teacher is well advised to plan several concerts, each featuring only one or two performing groups.

In planning the program itself, many conductors prefer to select first some outstanding work to serve as a high point and to build the rest of the program around it. This provides a climax for the concert, one memorable experience to make a deep impression on both student musicians and listeners, more likely to be remembered vividly and with pleasure than a program that either has no climax or is held to high levels of intensity throughout. By selecting one especially stimulating work and others that are relatively subordinate, the director considers the capacities for emotional response of the performers and the audience and the capabilities of young performers.

The concert may have subordinate climaxes and is in this respect similar to a dramatic performance. The principal climax may be preceded by others to set the mood and whet the appetite and may be followed by a lesser climax or one of a different type to avoid ending the concert too abruptly. If the concert includes one or more intermissions, it is appropriate that each segment have its own high point but that the different segments be unequal in intensity. The climactic work may be placed in the early portion of the concert, near its end, or close to the middle. If it makes heavy demands on the youngsters it may be necessary to place it near the beginning of the program so the group performs it before other selections have taxed their endurance. If the climactic work is of a lighter type and likely to prompt enthusiastic applause, it may be used as a final selection. If it is of a very serious nature noteworthy for musical beauty but quiet in mood, it may best be placed near the middle of the program so that other music may be used to prepare the mood of the singers and the audience and so it can be followed by selections that stimulate applause.

Planning in terms of climax, pupil capabilities, and audience response suggests a general pattern for a concert. The first selection is often for warm-up purposes. The members of the group must be given time to become accustomed to the stage, the unfamiliar lighting, and the knowledge that an audience is watching. More important, they must be given opportunity to flex their musical muscles and become accustomed to their sound in these unusual conditions before undertaking the performance of demanding music. A warm-up selection may be appropriate for the audience also, giving the listener time to settle in his seat and preparing him for the music to follow. For this purpose, the director chooses music that is easy to do, does not require extraordinary efforts of concentration by conductor, performers, or audience, and that functions as a curtain-raiser to arouse the enthusiasm of all concerned. He avoids subtleties of mood or style and turns instead to music that makes an immediate appeal, is colorful in harmony and has rhythmic vitality, but avoids exaggerated effects and extremes of range, dynamics, and ensemble precision.

As a next step in program building the director places the selection that is most demanding for all and is the high-point of the program. The logical place for music of this kind is in the early portion of the program, shortly before intermission. If the climactic work is not especially difficult to perform or for the audience to understand, it may better be placed later in the program, shortly after intermission, so that the audience retains a clear impression of it when the concert is over.

Immediately before intermission it is often desirable to present a short selection with strong audience appeal. Although those who attend public school concerts are in effect captive audiences and not likely to leave before the concert ends, it is well to stimulate their desire to hear more music and to provide strong incentive for them to return to their seats after intermission. This is especially desirable if more than one performing group participates in the program and if parents may feel content to leave after they have heard their children perform.

One reason for ending the first portion of the program with a flourish is that the segment before intermission is often longer than that which follows. If two halves of a program are of equal length, the second may seem unduly long and tiresome. Performers and audience are fresh and interested when the program begins, but they tend to become less able to concentrate on the music once intermission has passed. Thus the director plans a comparatively lengthy first half to take full advantage of the natural alertness of performers and listeners, but ends this portion of the program with a selection calculated to reawaken enthusiasm. A selection for this purpose should be short, vigorous, and exciting, productive of applause that leaves youngsters in high spirits and the audience eager to hear more.

For the first selection after intermission, the director may again choose music for warm-up purposes. The release of tension that follows successful performance and the fatigue felt by adolescents after they have concentrated their powers during the first half of a concert may find them even less ready to perform well after intermission than they were at the beginning of the program. A successful first half raises the spirits of the boys and girls, especially those of high school age, to such an extent that the second half of the program may suffer. The elation of having done well before an audience coupled with the volatile spirits of adolescents may cause them to forget much of what they had learned about the music to be done after intermission, to remove their attention from the conductor, and to perform too jubilantly with no control. Similarly, the audience may benefit from hearing music chosen to recapture the mood of the concert. These considerations suggest a selection that is short, rhythmic, and bold in its appeal, but compels the attention of the youngsters and requires control. This is followed by music lighter and more entertaining than that of the first half, chosen to hold the attention of musicians and audience and considerate of the young folks' lack of endurance.

To end the concert effectively the director chooses music especially impressive but not necessarily difficult. Depending upon the nature of the audience and the skill of the group, it might be either vigorous, rhythmic, and exciting or slow, hushed, and of serene beauty. A rousing number may be the best choice to stimulate enthusiasm and applause. In special circumstances or to vary the pattern of the concert program the director may find it effective to close with a quiet selection or a respectful presentation of the *alma mater*. The object in either case is to bring the concert to a memorable close, giving the ensemble and the audience an impressive music experience to carry away from the concert.

In determining the order in which the various selections are to be presented, the director continues to think in terms of variety and contrast. This may be a matter of keys, moods, tempos, music styles, or even the lengths of the various selections. The director can build the program in terms of a cycle of keys, following the lead of symphonic composers who begin and end their works in the same key and use contrasting but related keys for inner movements. A definite key scheme is seldom practical for the public school concert, but the director examines the key relations of successive selections nevertheless. In general he avoids the juxtaposition of several selections in the same key unless they are sufficiently different in mood to offer contrast to each other. He also avoids the other extreme of juxtaposing two selections of sharply different key. Two reasons for this are that the musicians' sense of tonality may be destroyed by a new and unrelated key, sufficient to influence intonation, and that the listeners' aural sense suffers a shock when the final chord of one selection is shattered by the opening tones of the next. Major and minor modes must be considered also, it being better in many instances to place a selection in minor mode between two in major rather than to place two minor modes together. Mood, tempo, and length are treated similarly, exciting music being followed by that which is quiet, fast by slow, short by long. The question of music styles may be treated somewhat differently. Here it is usually preferable to group selections of similar style together. Music of contemporary flavor or popular in nature does not mix well with that of the seventeenth and eighteenth centuries. With some exceptions, each type of music is most effective when presented with other selections of compatible style. Groups of different styles can be separated by intermissions, by a change in the seating arrangements of the chorus or in the instrumentation of the band or orchestra, or by interludes created in some other way.

There are many different patterns for the concert program, of course, the sequence of selections varying from concert to concert. In general, however, the principles described above merit consideration when any program is being planned. The director's goals might be summarized as follows:

1. To achieve unity through selection of a theme.

2. To provide variety and contrast through the succession of keys, moods, tempos, and lengths and the inclusion of music of different styles or historical periods.
3. To build around a high-point or series of climaxes.
4. To provide warm-up opportunities at the beginning of each segment of the program.
5. To provide a memorable conclusion for each portion of the concert.
6. To place difficult music in the early portion of the concert and be considerate of the youngsters' capabilities throughout.
7. To make the later portion of the concert shorter, lighter, easier to enjoy, and less demanding for performers and audience.
8. To limit the program to reasonable length and provide an intermission or other interlude when possible.

By following these precepts and adjusting them as necessary to fit each concert situation, the music teacher takes the first step in assuring that the program will be successful. If it is planned with care, the concert presented by even a newly formed group of inexperienced musicians can offer satisfaction to both participants and listeners, providing incentive for further musical development and the raising of standards in subsequent concerts.

The Printed Program

The printed program should show the date, time, and place of the concert and the name of the school and any other sponsoring organizations. The list of selections to be performed, composers, arrangers, soloists, accompanist, and suitable program notes are essential. Equally essential but sometimes overlooked are the names of participating members and all others who contribute to the success of the concert. Both pupils and parents are interested in seeing the roster of personnel and may save the program as a souvenir, and the teacher may find the list of members useful for reference in later years. Others who assist as dressing room supervisors, stage managers, ticket sellers, and ushers deserve mention. Their names should appear in the printed program as a matter of courtesy and to encourage their assistance at subsequent concerts.

Concert Acoustics

Many a splendid music program has failed because the director did not take care to check and recheck the acoustical conditions of the auditorium and stage before his performance there. A director should take no one's word on these matters; rather, he should let his own ear be the judge.

First, there is the stage on which the group performs. On some stages, sound disappears upward into the emptiness above the heads of the performers, while on others it is channeled into the wings. In either case it does not reach the audience. Some stages place the performing group in front of a hard-surfaced wall which reflects sound directly toward the audience, while others surround it with heavy draperies which absorb sound and deaden the stage. There may be live spots from which every whisper is audible in the last row of seats, or dead spots from which a flute player will be unheard regardless of how loudly he plays. Each of these possibilities is explored by the director before he uses any stage for the first time. Stage draperies can be raised or lowered to improve the acoustical effect. The performing group can be moved closer to the audience or closer to the rear wall. Sections and individual players can be shifted and the seating plan revised as necessary to improve balance. For many stages the best solution is the "box" set, a roomlike stage setting open on only one side with walls and ceiling made of painted canvas, plywood, or other materials. The box set functions as a shell, projecting all sound toward the audience, and is constructed so that it can be set up and dismantled easily. Several companies are now manufacturing lightweight acoustical shells specifically for bad stages and auditoriums. If a music teacher has a troublesome situation, he should look into the purchase of an acoustical shell immediately.

Second, there is the concert hall itself. Its acoustical properties are affected by its size and shape, the composition of walls, floor and ceiling, the area covered by window draperies and carpeting, and the number of people in the audience. The director judges hall acoustics by listening to the group from various places in the hall. Because he can usually do little to change the hall itself, he adjusts stage acoustics and the seating plan until he is content with the tonal effect. Because the effect may be quite different when the seats of the hall are filled with listeners, he regards his first adjustments as tentative. He listens again each time his group performs for an audience, continuing to adjust stage acoustics and seating until optimum balance, blend, and sonority are achieved.

Concert Showmanship

Showmanship is not a term that need be excluded from polite music conversation; it implies nothing more harmful than displaying one's wares in the best possible light. The term *wares* is used advisedly because music education has an important selling function—it must sell worthy music to as many people as possible. The fact that music is an art does not imply that it must be either esoteric or admired only from a distance. To the contrary, it is of value because it has meaning for all and because it is unique among the arts for its personal significance to the performer and the listener. It is proper that music education make every effort to promote the enjoyment of music and present it in the most favorable light. Doing so is helpful to the audience and provides benefits for those who teach or perform.

Showmanship is not out of place in concerts presented by public school ensembles. The concert can be made appealing to the eye as well as to the ear and entertaining as well as enjoyable in the aesthetic sense. To do so the teacher examines the techniques of television and Broadway, noting the devices used to capture audience interest and arouse enthusiasm, borrowing those appropriate to the concert.

The successful Broadway or television show is a model of effective showmanship. It utilizes all resources commensurate with good taste to sell its wares to the public, knowing that its life-span depends upon the size of the audience it attracts. Television has given millions of people repeated opportunities to see outstandingly entertaining programs compared with others that fail to win public approval, and it is not wise to offer a concert that appears dull, lifeless, and uninteresting when compared with standard television fare. This is not to imply that the serene beauty of masterpieces of musical art should be hidden under cheap costumes and gaudy makeup. Showmanship is offensive when it exceeds the limits of good taste or trespasses in areas reserved for the quiet contemplation of great beauty. Utilized properly and with good judgment it is a potent weapon with which music education can combat the influence of those forces in contemporary society which seem to be trying to crowd out the artistic dimension to life.

The colorful band has very little problem with showmanship. Its uniforms, its shiny instruments, its brilliant flags, its pretty majorettes—all contribute to the band's selling power. The orchestra suffers by comparison, but the orchestra still has the eye-catching motions of the players of the bowed instruments, and a few shiny instruments of its own. Orchestras would do well to copy some of the band's procedures: pins, ribbons, letters, awards, banquets, and the like.

The choir suffers most from a need for selling its concerts to the audience. Choral groups usually file on-stage in a disciplined manner and take seats in neatly arranged chairs or stand in orderly rows on choral risers. Beyond this there is little movement except when the choristers rise from their chairs to sing or file off the stage at the end of the program. This leaves the audience with very little to watch and provides little to hold visual attention. The chorus need not be visually static. Movement that holds the listener's visual attention helps hold his aural attention as well. A first step is to change the position of the chorus from one selection to the next. Form a compact group in the center of the stage, then change to a widespread arrangement that fills the space from wing to wing. Let one group of singers step forward for the selection that includes solos for their part. Place the various part-groups about the stage in a visually attractive arrangement. For one selection an echo choir in the rear of the auditorium or in the balcony might be suitable, whereas for another a group might sit cross-legged on the floor, on barrels and boxes, or dangle their legs from an improvised rail fence. There is the possibility of using carefully rehearsed gestures, of planning stage movements in the nature of choreography, or of inviting a dance group to participate in the concert by interpreting music sung by the chorus.

Choral concerts can be made visually interesting by varying the costume. The traditional uniform is the chorister's robe, a long, flowing garment of solid color and solemn effect. This is appropriate for the cathedral choir and for concerts presented on solemn occasions by the public school chorus, but it need not be the only costume in the choral wardrobe. It is inappropriate for some of the lighter music presented and provides little of visual interest to hold audience attention. A similarly formal but more interesting costume is dark suits for the boys and pastel dresses for the girls. Bright blazers or vests can be used to add color. Open-throated sport shirts and blouses combined with slacks or skirts may be suitable for some selections. Brightly colored rectangles of cloth can be used imaginatively as head coverings, scarves or shawls, sashes or apronlike skirts.

Special hats or gloves might be used to good effect. Even the traditional choral robe, purchased in one color for boys, a different color for girls, and with reversible stoles in contrasting colors can be used to provide visual variety. This is particularly effective if the boys stand in a compact group for one selection and mix with the girls to form quartets for the other. Original and often excellent ideas can be suggested by the pupils themselves for other costumes that can be devised at little or no expense, and the possibilities for using costume effectively to reflect the mood or text of the music and for varying it from one portion of the program to another give the choral director a means of holding audience interest.

Natural additions to stage movement and costumes are lighting, scenery, and props. Dramatic lighting can be used to intensify musical effect simply by changing colors from one portion of the program or one selection to the next. Spotlights focus attention on soloists, ensembles, or even on a tableau or decorative picture or object hung against a back-drop or over the heads of the chorus. Backdrops and scenery are more difficult to devise, but pieces once used for dramatic productions or made with the help of another department can sometimes be secured for special concerts. Props can be of any variety, from furniture moved from the teachers' room to articles brought from home by the singers. Lighting, of course, is the most convenient means of heightening the concert's visual appeal, but each of the other means should be explored and ex-perimented with by the teacher who wishes the choral concert to be an outstanding success.

Public performances by bands, choirs, and orchestras are an integral part of the American comprehensive high school. If the music director works at his responsibility with imaginative energy and good common sense, he can make an important contribution to the musical well being of the school and the community. He is, then, as he should be, more than a music director or conductor; he is a music educator in the full sense of the term.

PART IV

Instructional Tools, Techniques, and Materials

CHAPTER 9

Determining Musical Capacity and Achievement

Day in and day out a music teacher is asked to measure his students' work. He assigns solos, makes out tests, grades papers, gives out honors and awards, tests voices, marks report cards, and engages in all manner of objective and subjective appraisal of his students' potential and progress. It is the purpose of this chapter to review the instructional materials and techniques which have been used and which are being used by music educators in the above measurement tasks.

The terms *capacity* and *achievement* will occur, with their various synonyms, throughout the chapter quite frequently. *Musical capacity* is that proclivity for music which is found to some extent in every human being. *Capacity, innate musical ability, inherent aptitude, natural talent, native ability*, and similar terms appear interchangeably and indiscriminately in the literature. The general meaning is "potential for musical growth."

Achievement is just that—the demonstrable evidence of having grown, musically. Two tests are needed to measure achievement: one test before the instruction or exposure, one test after the instruction or exposure. *Achievement, development, growth, improvement, progress*, and similar terms are found in the literature in synonymic usage.

BACKGROUND

Musicians, psychologists, and educators are not in agreement on the nature of musical talent. Two schools of thought exist: (1) musical talent is a biological, inherited characteristic, and can no more be increased or cultivated than can eye color, hair texture, or nose structure; and (2) musical talent is a conditioned, environmental characteristic, and is subject to enormous cultivation and development. There is a great body of what seems to be scientific research to support each school.[1]

It is doubtful that the issue will ever be solved to anyone's satisfaction. It is an important issue, still, because it raises the question, "To what extent can a child be trained in music?" It is to this question that a music educator addresses himself every day of his career. The question is partially answered by the nature of the American public school system which takes the position that children can be trained in music to the extent that their proficiencies are quite acceptable to the community-at-large by the time the children reach high school.

In effect, this position puts music education as a profession in the environmental school with the behaviorists. Suffice, then, to offer suggestions for specific music education tasks in the area of testing, measuring, judging, diagnosing, grading, grouping, and so on, and to do so without regard to the nature-nurture issue at work in each situation.

IDENTIFYING TALENT FOR INSTRUMENTAL MUSIC

Among the applicants for instrumental instruction there are pupils who have interest but little or no talent. These students are often excluded from the instrumental program during the years in which it is attempting to produce acceptable performing groups with minimum resources. The inept pupil who is encouraged to begin instrumental study and perseveres through an extended period of lessons without achieving reasonable progress undergoes a frustrating experience. He becomes discouraged to such an extent that he may turn away from other forms of music activity in which he could find worthwhile satisfaction. Because of inevitable errors of judgment, inadequate testing, or circumstances beyond the control of the teacher, there are cases also in which the pupil withdraws from the instrumental program soon after he begins his study. The teacher does everything possible to prevent such cases by being careful in his selection procedure. The pupil suffers least disappointment if he is excluded from the program before he has acquired an instrument and before any instruction has been given. Permitting him to begin instrumental study wastes the teacher's time and prevents another pupil who may have

---

[1]For a general survey of the literature, see V. Horner, *Music Education: The Background of Research and Opinion.* Hawthorn, Victoria, Australia: Australian Council for Education Research, 1965, Chap. II, "Musical Abilities," pp. 14–64.

more talent from making good use of the instrument. Parents deserve consideration, too. It is important that children lacking in capability be identified before instruments have been purchased or rented. Finally, scheduling arrangements and the efficient use of the teacher's time demand that instrumental classes remain constant in size once they are established. The teacher's time is not used to best advantage if a class established at the beginning of a year is reduced to a fraction of its size by pupil withdrawals as the year progresses.

Even among the acceptable applicants for instrumental instruction there will be different degrees of talent that must be carefully evaluated. From this evaluation the teacher selects the instrument with which the pupil should begin and, at some later date, the instrument to which he might be transferred. He may search for pupils with an especially keen sense of pitch to encourage them to begin study of a stringed instrument. He might identify those with relatively weak pitch sense but strong rhythm and coordination, encouraging them to study percussion instruments. He selects those with adequate pitch and rhythmic sensitivity as well as good coordination for the various wind instruments. If complete and accurate information is gathered through tests administered at this early stage, the teacher may return to the test data at a later date to select pupils for transfer, for example, from clarinet to oboe or from trumpet to French horn.

Talent testing is one of the keys to a successful instrumental program. It is a species of diagnosis that establishes conditions favorable to the pupils' future progress. It helps assure that performing groups will be composed of competent players, each with the ability to understand and respond to music and the ability to master the instrument. It helps the teacher use his time and school facilities with maximum efficiency, providing instruction to pupils who can profit from it.

Talent discovery is another important aspect of the recruiting program, a process distinct from the testing of pupils who express interest in instrumental lessons. Some pupils with marked talent do not respond to the interest-arousing devices. It is unfortunate if these talented pupils are not encouraged to enter the program. As a case in point the author discovered a student in a college class who had been given no special training and who had not participated in music activities in earlier school years, but who had the unique sensitivity called absolute pitch! To one engaged in teaching music, this seems a tragic waste of talent. It is this sort of pupil the music teacher tries to identify as early as possible in the elementary school. It is imperative that they be discovered and proper that they be encouraged to develop their talent. Talent discovery may be regarded, therefore, as both an extension of the recruiting program and a normal function of music education. It reaches beyond the interested pupil to every member of the student body, seeking to identify those with extraordinary talent as well as those with lesser degrees of aptitude, encouraging them to begin participation of some sort in the instrumental program.

Informal Tests

The informal test devised by the teacher is desirable for a number of reasons. It can be adjusted to local conditions—to the size of the group taking the test, the age of the pupils to be tested, and the extent of their backgrounds and experience. It is often easier and quicker to administer than the standardized test. Answer sheets can be eliminated so that pupils of elementary school age are not hampered by the necessity of reading and writing terms they may not understand or following instructions that require abilities other than music talent.

There are two important factors to be discovered concerning a pupil's music potential. (1) Does he have rhythmic sense and sufficient muscular coordination to respond accurately to rhythm patterns? (2) Does he have sufficient pitch sense to judge and adjust intonation? Other factors such as tonal memory, aesthetic judgment, and sensitivity to degrees of loudness may be indicative of music talent also. It is believed, however, that pitch and rhythm are the factors of greatest interest to the instrumental teacher and that a test which measures these aspects of music talent provides an adequate basis for selecting pupils for beginning classes.

To test rhythmic sense the teacher turns to a testing procedure that utilizes rhythmic physical movement. One such test[2] is shown in Table 2. In this test the pupil is required to coordinate hand and foot movements in much the same way the beginning instrumental student learns to use his body in playing an instrument. He taps his foot to establish and maintain a rhythmic pulse and claps his hands to produce rhythm patterns indicated by easily read symbols. The letters "D" and "U" indicate motions of the toe as it moves "down" and "up," tapping the floor rhythmically to mark the pulse of the rhythm. The letter "x" written above the letters indicates that the pupil is to clap his hands at this point in the rhythm. The "x" occurs sometimes as the foot goes down, sometimes as it comes up, and there are lines in which there are two claps for each "D" or "U." Using this simple notation, the teacher can indicate a variety of rhythm patterns, including the simplest succession of quartet and half notes as well as complex patterns including sixteenth notes and syncopation.

---

[2]This procedure was suggested by Damon D. Holton, Director of Music, Norristown, Penn.

TABLE 2
Test for Rhythmic Coordination

```
    x              : x              : x              : x
1.  D  U  D  U  :  D  U  D  U  :  D  U  D  U  :  D  U  D  U
    x     x        : x     x        : x     x        : x     x
2.  D  U  D  U  :  D  U  D  U  :  D  U  D  U  :  D  U  D  U
    x  x  x  x     : x  x  x  x     : x  x  x  x     : x  x  x  x
3.  D  U  D  U  :  D  U  D  U  :  D  U  D  U  :  D  U  D  U
       x     x     :    x     x     :    x     x     :    x     x
4.  D  U  D  U  :  D  U  D  U  :  D  U  D  U  :  D  U  D  U
    x  x  x        : x  x  x        : x  x  x        : x  x  x
5.  D  U  D  U  :  D  U  D  U  :  D  U  D  U  :  D  U  D  U
    x  x     x     : x  x           : x  x     x     : x  x        x
6.  D  U  D  U  :  D  U  D  U  :  D  U  D  U  :  D  U  D  U
    x     x        : x  x  x        : x  x     x     : x  x
7.  D  U  D  U  :  D  U  D  U  :  D  U  D  U  :  D  U  D  U
    x x x x x      : x x x x x      : x x x x x x x: x x x x x
8.  D  U  D  U  :  D  U  D  U  :  D  U  D  U  :  D  U  D  U
    x  x x x       : x  x x x       : x  x x x       : x  x x x
9.  D  U  D  U  :  D  U  D  U  :  D  U  D  U  :  D  U  D  U
    x x x  x       : x x x  x       : x x x  x       : x x x  x
10. D  U  D  U  :  D  U  D  U  :  D  U  D  U  :  D  U  D  U
    x  x x x       : x x x x x      : x  x x x x x   : x  x  x
11. D  U  D  U  :  D  U  D  U  :  D  U  D  U  :  D  U  D  U
```

As a first step in administering the test, the teacher prepares the pupils by giving them an opportunity to practice the hand and foot movements. A large group of pupils can be led through this practice at one time. The symbols may be written on the board so that all may practice reading the test or, if the teacher anticipates reading difficulties, he may begin by asking the group to practice motions he demonstrates and describes verbally: In the latter case he might proceed as follows.

1. Tap your foot on the floor as I do. Be sure you can feel both the "down" motion and the "up" motion.
2. Tap your foot as you did before and clap your hands every time your foot goes down.
3. Tap your foot again. Clap your hands every time your foot goes down and every time it comes up.
4. Now clap every time your foot comes up, but do not clap when your foot goes down.
5. This time clap once when your foot goes down and twice when it comes up. Watch me as I show you how to clap this way.
6. Now clap twice when your foot goes down and only once when it comes up.

When the teacher feels the group has practiced enough to understand the tapping and clapping procedure, he places a number of exercises on the board. Both the rote practice and the written exercises can be adjusted to any level of difficulty the teacher thinks appropriate. Once the symbols are on the board, the teacher leads the entire group through the series of exercises, explaining and repeating lines as necessary to make certain the group understands the symbols and the desired motions. Although this procedure helps the pupil become familiar with the test procedure, it does not improve his response enough to overcome his deficiencies in rhythmic sense or coordination.

The next step is to test the pupils. They may be tested individually or in groups of six or more, preferably in a room away from the rest of those to be tested. In the test the pupils are asked simply to read the exercises on the board, tapping and clapping as they follow the symbols. The exercises may be the same as those used in the familiarization period, or new exercises of greater difficulty may be added. The teacher may again demonstrate certain exercises as necessary to help individual pupils who seem unable to coordinate their movements.

Although a test of this kind may not measure rhythmic sense as precisely or objectively as a standardized test, it does permit the teacher to judge the pupil's rhythmic aptitude for instrumental instruction. It uses symbols and movements similar to those the pupil must learn as he begins to play an instrument. The pupil is less likely to be confused by a test of this sort than by the answer sheets and formality of a standardized test. An entire class may be introduced to the test in from ten to twenty minutes, and small groups may be tested quickly without unduly disturbing the work of the balance of the class. With a minimum of experience the teacher learns to recognize the symptoms of lack of rhythmic sense and muscular coordination and can quickly identify the pupil who claps slightly before or after the beat or who cannot coordinate his movements. The pupil who cannot feel these rhythms or coordinate his movements is not a good prospect for instrumental lessons.

Equally simple and informal procedures are used to measure the pupil's pitch sense. Tests of different degrees of difficulty can be devised for pupils with different backgrounds and experience. Pupils who have been taught to use syllables or numbers in reading vocal music can be tested accordingly. For those with no such vocal instruction the test can be based on familiar songs. In either case the test requires the pupil to sing a series of pitches as directed by the teacher. The teacher listens to each child individually and judges whether he sings the pitches accurately and in tune. Here again the test relies on subjective judgment rather than accurate measurement. The teacher quickly discovers, however, that he can immediately identify pupils who sing in tune and those who seem to have little feeling for pitch. As he listens to pupils sing the test exercises, he can identify those who have begun to develop pitch sense also and can judge the desirability of exposing each pupil to special instrumental instruction.

The test itself can consist of one or several parts. First, the pupil may be asked to sing a phrase of one or more familiar songs. Suitable songs are those that are moderate in tempo, contain only simple and regular rhythm patterns, and offer both interval and scale passages to test the pupil's feeling for pitch. The teacher selects songs that have been taught in the music classes or that the child has learned outside of school. "America," "America the Beautiful," "Lovely Evening," "Brother John," and "Now Thank We All Our God" are examples of suitable songs. As the child sings the songs or phrases selected for the test, the teacher listens to determine whether he sings intervals accurately and moves with certainty from one scale tone to the next. The child who does not have pitch sense is apt to sing the second, third, and sixth tones of the scale out of tune and to be uncertain when he sings intervals of a third, fourth, or fifth.

A simple tonal memory is the next step in the procedure. The teacher dictates a series of four or more pitches or a short phrase, using the piano or some other instrument to produce tones in the child's vocal range. The child then sings the phrase as the teacher listens to determine whether he has remembered the series accurately and whether he sings each pitch and interval in tune. If the child is capable of responding by singing either syllables or numbers, he does so. If the child does not have this background he responds by singing neutral syllables.

The final step in the procedure is to test the child's feeling for scale relationships. This portion of the test requires the child to be familiar with some method of naming the tones of the scale—syllables, numbers, or letters. If these scale names have not been taught in other music work, the instrumental teacher may find that in some classes he can teach a portion of the scale ladder in a few minutes and that this brief introduction of scale names is sufficient to permit him to use this portion of the test. If these few minutes of teaching are not successful he simply eliminates this step of the testing procedure. For the test, he writes a portion of the scale ladder on the board as shown in Table 3, using whichever system of names is familiar to the pupils—syllables, numbers, or letters. He then dictates tonal groups to each pupil, sounding "Do" at the piano and then pointing to the pitches he wants the pupil to sing. He begins with an easy succession of pitches, such as "Do-Re-Do," and progresses to more difficult series such as "Do-Mi-Ti-Do." As the pupil sings the syllables in response, the teacher listens to determine whether he sings the tones in correct succession and whether each pitch is in tune. In this way he tests the pupil's aural imagery, tonal memory, pitch sense, and his feelings for scale relationships.

TABLE 3

Testing Aural Imagery Through Syllables, Numbers, Letters

Fa	4	F
Mi	3	E
Re	2	D
Do	1	C
Ti	7	B

A pitch test of this sort can be adjusted easily to the abilities of the groups to be tested. The teacher can add or delete exercises as necessary to challenge the talented pupil or to give the untalented pupil a feeling of accomplishment and success. The entire sequence of test exercises can be practiced in class prior to the test so that each child will understand the procedure when it is his turn to be tested. Small groups of from four to six pupils can be taken to a separate room for the test so that the balance of the class may continue its regular work.

To administer an informal rhythm and pitch test the teacher might proceed as follows:

1. Arrange to meet with either an entire class or a selected group of pupils who have expressed interest in instrumental music.
2. Briefly explain to the large group that each pupil is to be given a short, informal test to determine whether he is ready to begin instrumental lessons.
3. Lead the entire group through the rhythm test. Teach the movements first by rote and then read the test exercises from the board.
4. Lead the group through the pitch test. Sing the familiar songs or phrases selected for the test. Practice the tonal memory test by dictating from the piano for group response. Practice the scale relationships test by placing the scale ladder on the board and pointing to the tones sung by the group.
5. Arrange to have smaller groups of from four to six pupils sent to a separate room according to a schedule arranged with the classroom teacher.
6. In the testing room ask each pupil to read the rhythm exercises from the board. Then ask each pupil to sing the test song or phrase, to sing pitches dictated from the piano, and to sing pitch groups from the scale ladder.

7. Before pupils leave the testing room, interview each as necessary to determine family interest, instruments available, instrument desired, and so forth.

Through an informal test the teacher obtains information from which he can judge the pupil's aptitude for instrumental instruction. In some instances he can also form a tentative conclusion concerning the type of instrument with which the pupil might be successful. The test permits the teacher to have personal contact with each pupil. He can be alert for signs of nervousness or fatigue, giving individual help as necessary, and can ask for needed information as in an interview. The test is short and not conducive to fatigue or nervous tension. It does not require the pupil to read or write beyond his level of comprehension, and it does not tax his attention span in long periods of listening. Disadvantages are that it requires the personal attention of the instrumental teacher and permits the testing of only a few pupils at one time.

Standardized Tests

The standardized test does not offer the disadvantages of the informal test. Some can be administered by any music teacher, others by any teacher. Large groups of pupils can be tested at one time so that the test can be scheduled once for an entire school or grade without subsequent interruption of class work. Test construction is intended to eliminate subjective judgment through mechanical grading which can be done with a key by a person having no knowledge of music or of the test. There are established norms with which results can be compared and which permit easily understandable scores to be entered in the pupil's permanent record.

Standardized tests also offer certain disadvantages. Instructions and test procedures may be difficult for some pupils to understand. Answer sheets that require literary reading and writing may test the pupil's reading ability and powers of comprehension rather than his music talent. The test is sometimes long enough to exceed the pupil's attention span and cause fatigue even if given only a portion at a time. The test that relies on equipment such as the phonograph introduces mechanical difficulties having to do with the equipment itself, its operation, room acoustics, and so forth. Finally, some standardized tests are more difficult than necessary, exploring aspects and degrees of talent with which the instrumental teacher need not be concerned when selecting pupils for instrumental instruction.

In view of these disadvantages the instrumental teacher selects standardized tests with care. He writes to the publisher of each test to ask that a copy be sent for examination or for literature describing the test in detail. He may be able to secure one or more tests from local libraries or discuss the tests with teachers who have used them in neighboring communities. He studies each test carefully, perhaps even administering it to a small group of pupils. In the process he judges the test against local conditions to determine whether it meets his needs and is suitable for the pupils to be tested.

In evaluating the test the teacher first considers its validity. Does it measure what it is intended to test, or are results affected by other, nonmusical factors? Has its validity been measured by the authors or publishers? Is it reliable, that is, is it likely to be consistent in its results, giving the same evaluation for each pupil even if given more than once and despite unavoidable variations in test conditions? Must it be administered all at one time, or could it be given a portion at a time to reduce fatigue? Are answer sheets easy to understand and complete, or do they require well-developed abilities to read, write, and understand? Is special equipment required by the test, and is suitable equipment available in schools in which the test is to be used? Can the test be administered and marked by any teacher, or must the instrumental teacher give it his personal attention? Even though many such questions have been investigated by the test authors, each instrumental teacher asks them again in the light of his own complete knowledge of his needs and the conditions peculiar to his own school system.

After investigating all the tests to which he has access, the instrumental teacher is ready to select those appropriate for his testing program. He may choose one for all pupils or several to be used at different grade levels or for different groups. He may select single portions of several different tests, combining them to form one test meeting his special requirements. He may devise his own answer sheets, adjusting them to the abilities of the pupils to be tested, and may adjust the length and difficulty of the tests themselves. In doing so he may create a new test to which established norms do not apply, a sacrifice compensated for by the increased usefulness of the test in his music program.

The following is a list of tests available to the instrumental teacher, designed to measure music talent and the pupil's potential as an instrumental player.

Drake Musical Aptitude Tests, Raleigh M. Drake. Distributed by Science Research Associates, 57 West Grand Ave., Chicago, Ill.

Tests for (1) rhythm, (2) musical memory. Age eight to adult. Includes examiner manual, self-scoring answer pads, one microgroove 33 1/3 rpm recording.

Kwalwasser Music Talent Test. Jacob Kwalwasser. Distributed by Mills Music, Inc., 1619 Broadway, New York, N.Y.

Two tests: Form A, junior high school through college; Form B, children through grade six. Includes instruction manual, test blanks, scoring key, one 78 rpm recording (tones produced by electronic instruments).

Measures of Musical Talent. C. E. Seashore. Distributed by Psychological Corporation, 522 Fifth Ave., New York, N.Y.

Tests for (1) pitch, (2) intensity, (3) time, (4) consonance, (5) tonal memory, (6) rhythm. Recommended for grades five through eight. Includes manual of instructions, test blanks, six 78 rpm recordings.

Musical Aptitude Test (Series A). Harvey S. Whistler and Louis P. Thorpe. Distributed by California Test Bureau, 5916 Hollywood Blvd., Hollywood, Calif.

Tests for (1) rhythm recognition, (2) pitch discrimination, (3) advanced rhythm recognition. Grades four through ten. Includes instruction manual, answer sheets. (No record. Examiner plays examples at piano.)

Test of Musicality, 4th ed. E. Thayer Gaston. Distributed by Odells Instrumental Service, 925 Massachusetts St., Lawrence, Kan.

Grades four through twelve. Includes manual of directions, scoring key, test form, one 33 1/3 rpm recording.

Wing Standardized Tests of Musical Intelligence. Herbert D. Wing and Cecelia Wing. Distributed by the National Foundation for Educational Research, 79 Wimpole St., London, England.

Tests for (1) chord analysis, (2) pitch change, (3) memory, (4) rhythmic accent, (5) harmony, (6) intensity, (7) phrasing. Grades three and above.

Several manufacturers of music instruments also have musical aptitude tests on the market. These tests must be used with reserve because they tend to be fairly short and easy, and an inordinate number of the students get high scores.

Other Information Sources

Additional information about each pupil can be obtained from other sources. Vocal teachers are familiar with the pupil's general music ability, singing ability, and interest in music, all of which are directly pertinent to the selection of instrumental beginners. Classroom and homeroom teachers know whether the pupil is quick to learn, interested in school work, dependable in his work habits, and generally successful in his school work.

They often know whether he comes from a musical home and whether his parents might look favorably on extra music instruction. Permanent record cards maintained by each school show test scores dealing with such factors as intelligence, aptitudes, and interests. They offer a complete scholarship record showing degrees of success in various subject areas as well as a record of participation in extracurricular and out-of-school activities and comments concerning the pupil's conduct. They give information about the pupil's parents, their occupations, socio-economic status, and other conditions in the home.

All this information is of use to the instrumental teacher. He collects as much as he can before reaching a decision about each pupil. He considers the pupil's talent as indicated by rhythm, pitch, and standardized tests. He consults other teachers to ask their opinions about the pupil's music potential and general character. He searches for pertinent data in permanent school records. Ultimately, he talks with the parents of the pupils he has identified as likely prospects. With the information derived from all these sources he is equipped to make informed judgments and to select pupils who will profit from instrumental instruction.

This data-collecting process involves many steps and is important to the success of the pupil and of the instrumental program. The teacher therefore establishes a carefully conceived testing program as a regular part of the annual school calendar. It includes a sequence of steps that recurs automatically year after year and requires only minimum effort on the part of music and other teachers.

A talent test is administered each year to all pupils in a particular grade. The intent is to test every pupil who passes through the school system and to identify talented pupils before instrumental classes are formed. Every pupil is then retested one or two years later to make certain no talented pupil was overlooked during the first testing. This step is highly desirable. Teachers often find that a significant number of pupils who ranked low in the first test—due to nervousness, minor illness, or some unidentifiable cause—achieve markedly higher scores when retested. Either the same or a different test may be used. When scheduling arrangements permit, both tests are given in the spring so that the organized classes may begin promptly at the beginning of the next school year.

Scores or anecdotal comments are entered in the pupil's permanent record, and further information is gathered at the same time from the permanent records, other music teachers, and classroom teachers. This gives the instrumental teacher complete information about each pupil who ranked high in the tests and permits other teachers to suggest the names of pupils who might benefit from special instruction despite low test scores. With this information available the instrumental teacher is able to identify likely prospects for instrumental classes. He can write appropriate letters to parents of children who scored high in the tests, talk with the pupils, and make plans for the necessary beginners' classes.

CLASSIFYING VOICES: JUNIOR HIGH SCHOOL

Although it is necessary for practical purposes to define the voice ranges of adolescent singers and to group them in categories, each voice is unique in quality and range. It is erroneous to think of voices as being all alike, or to assume that voices can be separated into a few groups of identical range and quality. For the purposes of the general music class and of singing activities in general, it is necessary to arrive at a satisfactory criterion for grouping similar voices so the parts assigned will be within the vocal compass of each singer in the group. This is especially difficult to accomplish where adolescents are concerned because of the relatively narrow compass of some voices and the frequency with which vocal ranges change.

Register and Compass

As an indication of the marked change in register occurring in boys' voices, and the relatively minor change in girls' voices, Example 1 shows the differences between ranges of adult men and women and those of boys and girls at the age of ten, prior to voice change. These data from Jersild and Bienstock[3] include information concerning the pitches produced by children younger than ten years of age, both boys and girls. The extremes of range shown include all pitches the tested individuals were able to produce, including those of the man's falsetto voice, and are pitches produced alone rather than in the context of a song or some other vocal line. The ranges shown, therefore, are not necessarily those throughout which the test subjects were able to sing easily and well. Pitches at the high and low extremes may have been beyond comfortable singing compass, of faulty tone quality, and produced with extreme vocal strain. The information is revealing:

1. The voices of boys and girls expand similarly in compass until they reach approximately nine years of age.

---

[3] Arthur T. Jersild and Sylvia F. Bienstock, "A Study of the Development of Children's Ability to Sing," *Journal of Educational Psychology*, XXV, No. 7 (1934), 491. This research is dated, but it has since been substantiated. See Horner, *op. cit.*, pp. 115–16.

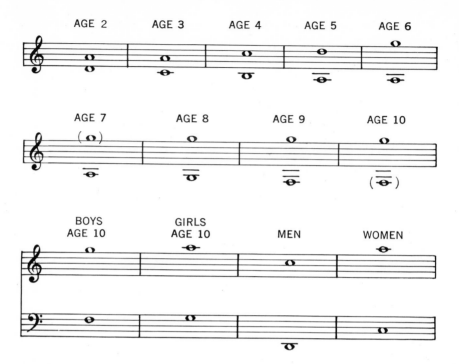

Example 1 Voice ranges of children and adults. Pitches not in parentheses were produced by 50 percent, pitches in parentheses by 48–50 percent of total individuals tested. Range for men includes the falsetto.

2. The voices of boys and girls begin to show slight differences in range at age ten or soon thereafter.
3. The compass of girls' voices expands downward, but not upward, as the voice matures.
4. The voices of boys drop approximately one octave during voice change.

Frequently Used Terms

The literature dealing with adolescent voices uses a variety of terms to identify ranges and qualities. The differences of opinion among various authors testify to the difficulty of establishing categories suitable for all voices. Example 2 summarizes these terms. Some are normal to vocal literature written for mature voices; others are appropriate only to changing voices.

The problem of range is a complex one. It is possible to describe their variety more completely by increasing the number of range classifi-

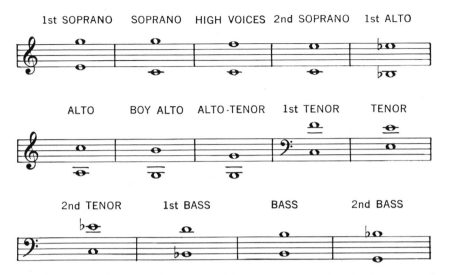

Example 2 Classifications and ranges cited in various texts to describe the variety of adolescent voices.

cations, but this increase in categories does little to solve the teacher's problem of using adolescent voices in the song material available. What, then, is the teacher to do? The principal objective is to find a place for every voice in the singing activities of the class. To accomplish this the teacher must test each voice to discover its range limitations, must examine the available song literature to discover its range demands, and on the basis of this information must assign voices to parts each can sing without discomfort.

Demands of the Literature

As an indication of what the teacher may meet in analyzing song literature, Example 3 summarizes the findings of a random sampling of song materials intended for use with changing voices in the junior high school; Example 4 presents data from a similar sampling of books for use with changed voices in the senior high school. To collect these data, many songs were selected at random from appropriate songbooks. Each voice part in each song was examined to determine what range the singer would need to sing that voice part. In these figures the two note heads in each "measure" are the highest and lowest pitches in one voice part of one song.

As indicated by Example 3, song literature available to the teacher in the junior high school permits the use of voices of many registers and

Example 3 Compass of voice parts in songs selected at random from books intended for use with changing voices in the junior high school. (The two note heads in each measure show the highest and lowest pitch in one voice part of one song.)

compasses. Unison songs and parts for higher treble voices offer compasses of from less than one octave to as much as a twelfth, occasionally rising to two-line G or descending to small B-flat.[4] Parts for medium voices may vary from a fourth to an octave or more in compass, with two-line D and small A as their upper and lower extremes. Lower voices of both boys and girls may be assigned to parts of from a fourth to a tenth in compass, descending as far as small G. Boys with changing voices may

_____

[4]Pitches are referred to here as being in the great octave, small octave, one-line octave, or two-line octave, these octaves beginning, respectively, two octaves below middle C, one octave below middle C, at middle C, and one octave above middle C.

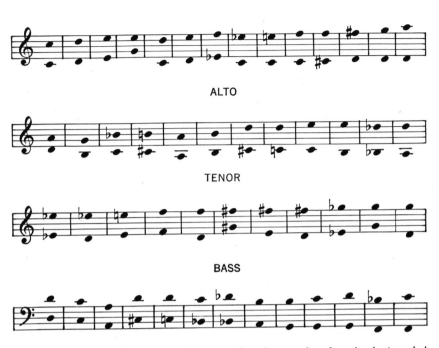

Example 4 Compass of voice parts in songs selected at random from books intended for use with changed voices in the high school. (The two note heads in each measure show the highest and lowest pitch in one voice part of one song.)

be assigned to parts as narrow in compass as a fourth or fifth and rarely more than an octave, all centered around middle C. Boys with changed voices may be assigned to bass parts of from a fifth to a tenth in compass, but rarely descending further than great A. In this variety of ranges and registers there is something suitable for voices in almost every stage of voice change.

The literature for changed voices, as indicated by Example 4, is more demanding. Here there are fewer songs in which the compass of voice parts is an octave or less. Sopranos, altos, tenors, and basses are assumed to have developed the ability to sing through a compass of a twelfth or or more, the separate parts approaching the difficulty of those intended for mature, trained voices. There are some arrangements in which each part remains within an octave, but it would be extremely difficult to find enough literature of this sort to meet the demands of the general music class. As a general rule, it is easier to find appropriate song literature in books intended for use with changing voices.

A Workable Solution

To use adolescent voices properly, the teacher of general music begins testing voices. In testing, it is the teacher's objective to discover the register and compass of each voice and to establish a relatively small number of range categories for grouping all the voices of the class. To facilitate the assignment of parts, the compass of each category should be narrow enough to permit all voices in the group to sing throughout the entire compass without strain, and each category should be wide enough in compass to include enough voices for satisfactory singing of parts in the song literature. This is an ideal which is sometimes difficult to achieve. Each class is different from the others, and the voices in any one class change in register and compass with dismaying rapidity. The alternative of asking pupils to refrain from singing when their voices are not equal to the demands of the literature tends to defeat the purpose of the general music class.

The second step is to examine the available song literature. Here it is the teacher's objective to determine the compass of each song or each vocal part, and to select those suitable for the range categories established through voice testing. Although this can be a time-consuming process, it is made easier by the teacher's experience and by the fact that the number of songbooks and other materials usually available for use in the general music class is relatively small. If the teacher keeps written records of this analysis in a card index, notebook, or on the flyleaf of each songbook, showing the page numbers of songs suitable for each vocal category, the list of appropriate materials grows month by month and year by year, ultimately ending the need for further analysis.

TESTING VOICES: JUNIOR HIGH SCHOOL

From the foregoing discussion of ranges it is obvious that voice testing is one of the teacher's important responsibilities and that it must be done carefully and accurately. The voice test must be appropriate to the nature and objectives of the general music class. The aim is to nurture voices, not to force them into what the teacher believes to be proper choral balance. Choral balance is desirable, but the welfare of each voice is of paramount importance, and choral balance is sacrificed if individual voice characteristics do not permit a balance of choral parts.

In the general music class it is appropriate to depart from the usual concept of the voice test as a means of determining quality rather than range. Where professional singers or trained choral groups are concerned, it is proper to classify voices on the basis of voice quality to ensure, for example, that alto parts are sung with alto quality. Where adolescent singers are concerned, it is more important that changing voices be assigned to parts they can sing comfortably than that any one voice part be homogeneous in quality. The voice test, therefore, is a means of determining register and compass, vocal quality being of secondary importance until the voices of the group have matured sufficiently to sing standard voice parts without difficulty.

Because adolescent voices change rapidly, voice tests are given on a regular basis at least twice each year, more often when the progress of voice change in the class warrants further testing. In addition to the regular testing of entire groups, individual voices are retested whenever it becomes difficult for the pupil to sing with the group to which he has been assigned.

To test large groups efficiently it is necessary to establish a test procedure, to describe it briefly to the class before testing is begun, and to adhere to the established procedure in all subsequent tests. This makes the task much easier for the teacher, facilitates quick but accurate testing of large numbers of voices, helps avoid embarrassment for pupils reluctant to display their changing voices, and contributes materially to class discipline and control. In some respects voice testing is the cornerstone of singing activities in the general music class. Correct voice classification protects adolescent voices, permits progress in the vocal work of the class, and is conducive to the success in singing which encourages interest and participation.

Testing Individuals

The most accurate voice-testing procedure is one in which each voice is heard individually and sufficient time is allotted to permit complete exploration of each pupil's vocal capabilities. In some few instances the teacher may be able to arrange individual tests before or after school or during free periods. Once pupils of the general music class have become accustomed to the teacher, to each other, and to voice-testing procedures, it may be feasible in some classes to conduct individual voice tests during class time. If so, it is desirable to move the piano to the rear of the room, turning it so that the back of the pupil being tested is to the backs of those in their seats and so that the teacher at the piano can see the class as well as the pupil being tested. In addition, it is necessary that all pupils in the room be given assigned work, preferably of a written nature, to engage their attention during the testing period.

In view of the adolescent's normal reluctance to sing alone, it is not advisable to attempt individual testing until each class is well under control and until each pupil understands the necessity for voice testing and is curious about his own vocal progress. On the whole, individual testing requires experience in class management on the part of the teacher and well-developed cooperative attitudes on the part of pupils. It is to be avoided by the inexperienced teacher or by any teacher who has not won the complete cooperation of the class.

Testing Small Groups

A procedure somewhat less accurate, but more appropriate to the general music class, is one in which voices are tested in small groups. In this procedure, from four to six pupils gather at the piano at one time, singing as a group except when the teacher finds it necessary to ask individuals to sing alone, briefly, to check accurately some factor of register or compass. In this procedure, as in the previous one, every effort is made to ensure privacy for those being tested and to establish circumstances favorable to class control. The piano can be moved to the rear of the room or turned so that pupils being tested do not face those at their seats. Pupils at their seats need assigned work as well as the visual attention of the teacher.

The first step in determining vocal register is to listen to the speaking voice of each pupil. Boys, especially, show the effects of voice change in their speaking voices. The teacher can often make accurate preliminary judgments from listening to the boy give his name or answer a routine question. This is done prior to voice testing, if possible, so that the teacher may have some general basis for selecting voices of similar register to make up each test group.

To begin testing, the teacher plays a familiar song, asking the pupils of the group to sing with the piano. The best songs for this purpose are those of limited melodic compass, based on relatively simple harmonic patterns, and well known to all members of the class. The first phrase of "America," for example, requires pupils to sing only through the narrow compass of a diminished fifth, can be transposed easily by the teacher into a number of different keys, and is well known to all pupils. Because the melody is familiar and easy to sing, pupils begin singing with little hesitation. By transposing this melodic fragment into different keys the teacher can explore the upper and lower limits of voices being tested.

If the teacher is not content with the information obtained through the use of a familiar song or melodic fragment, it is possible to use short scale passages. These provide a better measure of the upper and lower extremes of the voices, need extend only through the compass of a fourth or fifth, and should be sung by the group to the accompaniment of an interesting harmonic pattern. The short scale patterns and their harmonic accompaniments, like the melodic fragment, can be transposed by the teacher as needed to extend the span of the test, probing further and further into the extremes of vocal range.

In this process it is important that the entire group of pupils being tested sing together, that they sing always with the support of the piano, and that the piano accompaniment be appealing to adolescent tastes. The teacher, face to face with only a small group of pupils, is able to hear each of the voices in the group as they sing together, noting the pitch at which any voice stops singing or begins to show signs of strain. The pupils in the group, even boys in the most awkward stage of voice change, feel relatively at ease among others with similar vocal characteristics. They are never asked to sing without the piano and seldom without the vocal support of the balance of the group, are asked to sing only familiar passages of narrow compass, and may even find the testing enjoyable if the teacher shows imagination in creating attractive piano accompaniments.

When testing voices it is almost inevitable that the teacher will discover one or more pupils who have difficulty finding the pitch at which the other members of the group begin singing. For these changing voices of limited range, the teacher begins by finding a pitch that can be sung, then expands the range from that point to determine how far above and how far below the first pitch the pupil can sing. Here, even more than in other parts of the test, the teacher provides support for the uncertain singer through piano accompaniment and the singing of the other members of the group. Adolescents who have this singing difficulty usually respond better when tested among a group of friends. They are more in need of support than the accomplished singers, and far more in need of the teacher's close attention, careful testing, and correct voice-part assignment.

Testing Large Groups

In some general music classes even the foregoing method of group testing is impractical because of pupil attitudes and problems of class control. In others it is desirable to test voices during the first few meetings of the class, before the teacher has had time to stimulate interest in singing or to win class support and cooperation. Here there is need for a means of testing voices quickly without drawing special attention to any one singer or even to a small group of pupils who must sing while the major portion of the class is silent.

One such process[5] is intended for use in the junior high school. It assumes that voices of adolescent girls are more or less uniform in range and that most girls can sing either first or second soprano parts. This implies that girls' voices need not be tested and that the teacher's first duty is to identify unchanged, changing, and changed voices among the boys.

To test the boys' voices, the teacher first asks all boys to sing "Old Folks at Home" in the key of B-flat, identifying as baritones all those able to sing it in the lower octave. These changed voices are then instructed to remain silent as the rest of the boys sing "Old Folks at Home" in the key of G-flat. In this key the boys able to sing in the upper octave are unchanged voices (sopranos), and the balance are changing voices (cambiata). Although this procedure does not permit the teacher to test voices carefully or accurately, it has obvious merit in that it solves the problem of initial voice classification without placing any pupil in the focus of class attention.

After voices have been tested the teacher seats the class according to voice classifications, placing like voices together in any seating plan that facilitates singing activities. Two general rules govern this seating: (1) place uncertain singers near the piano so that they may take full advantage of its support; (2) place boys near the teacher so that their natural exuberance may be more easily controlled. If these two rules are followed, girls are seated toward the rear of the room, higher voices toward one side and lower voices toward the other. Boys with unchanged voices sit immediately in front of the girls, similarly separated in terms of higher and lower voices. Boys with changing voices sit toward the front of the room, grouped in seats closest to the piano. Boys with changed voices are seated near the piano also, and toward the front of the room, grouped next to the boys with changing voices.

If there are pupils of any voice classification who find it difficult to match pitches, it is usually helpful to surround each of them with experienced singers. In some instances boys' attitudes improve when they are separated from each other and interspersed among the girls, but in general, they seem to be more at ease in the music class when seated together.

CLASSIFYING VOICES: SENIOR HIGH SCHOOL

As an indication of the wide variety of voice ranges and qualities, Table 4 lists some of the terms used to classify voice types. Ranges given are

[5]Irvin Cooper, *Letters to Pat Concerning Junior High School Vocal Problems*. New York: Carl Fischer, Inc., 1953, pp. 19–20. For a full treatment of Cooper's method of voice classification, see Irvin Cooper and Karl O. Kuersteiner, *Teaching Junior High School Music*. Boston: Allyn and Bacon, 1965, pp. 29 ff.

generalizations only, necessarily ignoring the variations among individuals of the same classification in order to reduce the list to reasonable length. Despite the large number of descriptive terms in common use, it is difficult to find a term that describes precisely the range and quality of an

TABLE 4
Voice Classifications, Ranges, and Characterisics

Classification	Range	Description
Soprano	c^1 to a^2	Characterized by brightness of quality and ringing tone
Coloratura soprano	e^1 to f^3	Agile voice suited to execution of coloratura embellishments
Lyric soprano	c^1 to c^3	Light voice of pure quality suited to cantabile style
Dramatic soprano	c^1 to c^3	Voice with power and brilliance suited to declamatory roles
Mezzo-soprano	b-flat to b-flat^2	A voice both rich and bright, combining characteristics of soprano and contralto
Mezzo-contralto	g to g^2	Light contralto quality midway between contralto and mezzo-soprano
Contralto	e to e^2	Rich and full, especially weighty in lower register
Haute contre	c to c^2	Term now largely obsolete, denoting high tenor
Tenor	c to c^2	Characterized by brightness of tone and ringing quality
Lyric tenor	d to c^2	Light voice of pure quality suited to cantabile style
Heroic tenor	c to c^2	Powerful, brilliant, and agile, suited to dramatic roles
Tenore robusto	c to c^2	Characterized by fullness, vigor, and power of tone
Tenor-baritone	B-flat to b-flat^1	Combining tenor and baritone characteristics and midway between them
Baritone	A-flat to a-flat^1	Fullness of quality with depth in lower register, brightness above
Bass-baritone	G to f-sharp^1	A voice with depth and power, especially effective in lower register
Basso cantante	G to g^1	A low voice of lyric quality suited to cantabile style
Basso buffo	F to e^1	A low but agile voice suited to roles of comic nature
Basso profondo	C to c^1	Characterized by resonance of its lower register
Contra-bass	F_1 to c^1	Doubly low

individual voice, especially when dealing with adolescents whose voices are not yet fully developed.

The teacher's first step is to reduce the list of voice types to those customarily used in reference to adult singers: soprano, mezzo-soprano, contralto, tenor, baritone, and bass. Where professional singers are concerned, it is normal to expect a voice compass of two octaves or more, but it is advisable to expect a compass of slightly less than two octaves, perhaps a thirteenth, when dealing with untrained singers. As a means of comparison, adult voices might be regarded as having a compass that extends seven tones above and seven tones below the pitches d, f, and a for basses, baritones, and tenors respectively, e^1, g^1, and b^1 for contraltos, mezzo-sopranos, and sopranos. For choral work, these categories may be reduced to four by the elimination of the mezzo-soprano and baritone classifications. The remaining classifications—soprano, alto, tenor, and bass —provide a basis for assigning adult voices to choral parts, subdivided if necessary for eight-part music. Two other factors are voice quality, having to do with resonance, weight, and color of tone, and *tessitura*, the area within the vocal compass in which the voice can be used most comfortably.

Once these classifications are established, it is the teacher's responsibility to select appropriate materials, rejecting the selections that carry any part beyond the established limits. The teacher is well advised to establish a set of classifications for each choral group, based upon both voice testing and a survey of the appropriate literature; the requirements for the middle voice in a group singing SAB arrangements, for example, would be different from those of the lowest voice in a group singing SSA arrangements. Moreover, the teacher will find it desirable to establish classifications appropriate for the pupils in his own school rather than to accept criteria developed in a different situation; voice ranges and classifications are likely to vary from urban to rural areas and to be affected by other factors in such a way that standards satisfactory in one school are quite unsatisfactory in another.

The classification of senior high school voices may proceed, generally, along lines similar to those established for classifying junior high school voices. Senior high school voices are somewhat more matured than those of pupils in the junior high school, but they still are not developed to the point of adult range and quality. It is thus unwise to assume that high school pupils can be tested and classified according to criteria established for adults; to the contrary, it is essential that the teacher develop a concept of reasonable range through experience in testing voices and through analysis of literature to be sung.

Example 4, page 165, indicates the range demands of choral literature intended for high school singers. Most of the literature can be sung by voices with a compass of one and a half octaves, a fact that provides a basis for voice classification. The teacher might establish these ranges arbitrarily, noting each individual's ability to sing beyond the established compass or his difficulty in singing either its upper or lower extreme: soprano c^1 to g^2; alto a to e^2; tenor c to g^1; bass G to d^1. Parts are then assigned according to these criteria, and music is selected to fit the capabilities of the singers. In some instances the teacher will find that the soprano range can be extended to a^2 or the bass to F. In others it may be useful to regard the group as being composed of eight parts to permit more accurate classification of voices. In the event it is desirable for some special reason to prepare a choral selection that exceeds the established ranges, one that requires altos to sing down to g, for example, the teacher must decide which voices shall be permitted to sing the part and whether there are enough able voices to make performance feasible.

TESTING VOICES: SENIOR HIGH SCHOOL

One of the basic questions concerning current practices in music education, particularly at the high school level, is whether music should be for all or only for the talented. If the performing group is closed to those who have comparatively little skill, it becomes a specialized organization that does not minister to the needs of all who would benefit from it. It is obvious that the level of performance rises when requirements for entrance are highly selective; the better the performer, the better the performance. It is not proper, however, to deny students of average or less-than-average singing ability the opportunity to sing in some kind of ensemble, however small or modest it may be. For this reason, high schools have several choirs and glee clubs. There should be one organization which accepts any and all who apply. This group, however, should strive for the highest performance standards at all times.

Test Goals

Whether the teacher's intent is to select talented singers or to determine the ability of all who apply, the tryout procedure explores thoroughly the characteristics of each voice and the ability of each singer. The teacher must have accurate and complete information about the pupil if he is to be assigned to the proper part and to gain from his choral experience. There is a stronger need for careful testing of the weaker singer than of those who are outstanding. To guide the pupil properly, the teacher should know each singer well:

1. Vocal range, including both the register and compass of the voice.

2. Voice quality, including beauty of tone and suitability for a particular part.
3. Pitch accuracy, including sensitivity to blend and tonal memory.
4. General musicianship and sensitivity to musical effect.
5. Music-reading ability, including understanding of notation, and the ability to hold a part in an ensemble.
6. Character, including attitude, interest, and dependability.

Each of these factors is pertinent to the teacher's problem of understanding, placing, and guiding the pupil and to the degree of success he will enjoy as a member of the choral group. The means of gathering this information are varied. Each teacher must develop a testing procedure in accordance with his own preferences, the characteristics of the pupils being tested, and the standards established for the choral ensemble.

Planning the Procedure

When testing applicants for a glee club intended to stimulate interest and provide for large numbers of pupils, the teacher might decide to use nothing more than a test for range, drawing conclusions about other factors during the course of this one test. For an advanced and more selective choir, the teacher determines range, quality, pitch sensitivity, and musicianship with considerable accuracy. For small ensembles, all factors are important, including the manner in which the voice blends with others in a quartet. In every case the test procedure is determined by the nature of the group being formed, the general level of abilities among applicants, and the time available for testing. It is important also that the teacher develop a system for conducting the test once its content has been determined, establishing a pattern that can be followed with every pupil to prevent waste of time. If it is possible to meet all applicants in one group before voice tests are conducted, the teacher can ensure that testing will proceed smoothly and swiftly by explaining the nature of the test and by asking pupils to sing the test exercises together before singing them individually.

Time-Saving Devices

Voice testing requires a great deal of the teacher's time if it is to be done properly, but the teacher's load can be markedly reduced through advance planning and systematic procedures. Voice tests can be conducted in the spring of one year for choral groups that are to be active during the next. This prevents the loss of several weeks for testing during the beginning of the year when rehearsal time must be used to greatest advantage. It also permits the teacher to conduct tests without conflict with the activities natural to the beginning of the school year and without competing for the attention of pupils trying to become accustomed to new classes, teachers, and perhaps a new school.

In setting dates for the voice-testing period the teacher first checks his own schedule for performances and other responsibilities and the school calendar to avoid conflict with examination periods and other special events. It is advisable to arrange for testing voices of interested pupils in the final year of nearby elementary or junior high schools. For this, the teacher secures the approval of the principal and enlists the cooperation of the music teacher in the lower grade. Tests are given by scheduled appointment, the teacher posting appointment sheets on the bulletin board to permit pupils to sign their names after preferred times. This requires the teacher to estimate the time needed for his test procedure, establish a testing schedule, and adhere to it to utilize the available time efficiently.

A mimeographed form is a useful time-saving device. File cards, perhaps 5 x 7 inches, are desirable because they are easy to file. The form might provide space for data from cumulative records, coded as necessary to prevent disclosure of confidential information to pupils, questionnaire items to be completed by the pupil, giving complete name, address, telephone, training, experience, and other desired information, and a series of items to be checked by the teacher during the voice test to record voice range, quality, intonation, and so forth. One form might be prepared in advance for each student who signs the appointment sheet and the questionnaire items completed immediately before or after the pupil is given the voice test. The teacher might further reduce the burden of this work by selecting a student assistant, an officer or member of the choral group for which tests are being conducted. The assistant is given the responsibility of ushering pupils in and out of the testing room at their appointed times, answering questions as applicants complete questionnaires, and doing other clerical work to free the teacher for the more important work of testing voices.

THE CHALLENGE SYSTEM

Directors of instrumental music sometimes allow their students to test and place each other in the ensemble. The "challenge system" permits any student to try to play more proficiently than the person sitting above him in the section. If he succeeds, he takes the chair of the one he has successfully challenged. He is then permitted to challenge again. He goes until he decides to stop, or until he fails to gain the chair he sought.

The system usually generates quite a competitive spirit in the sections, and some means of control must be established. Challenges should not occur indiscriminately at any time; it is best to set aside one day every two weeks, perhaps, for the challenges, even if an entire period is consumed at the time. The system works best if the student who is second in line is given first chance to challenge. Should he fail, the third in line is given a chance to challenge him, and so on. There should be no challenges that jump over a chair; the ambitious challenger must work his way up through the entire section if he hopes to capture first chair.

The most popular challenge system is one in which the students determine if the challenger has unseated the challenged. The students are asked to close their eyes and to raise their hand for the student whose performance was best. Directors who use this system claim that the students are brutally honest in their voting, that they will vote their best friend down a chair if a challenger plays more proficiently, and they will vote an otherwise unpopular student right up to the top and keep him there as long as he holds his own against the challengers below.

TESTING FOR ACADEMIC ACHIEVEMENT

When a teacher-prepared written test is in order, it should follow certain principles. These principles will be of assistance to the new music teacher confronted with his first need for a written test of his own making.

Physical makeup:

1. The test should be reproduced clearly and accurately with all sections easily readable.
2. Directions should be simple and complete, with perhaps an example for illustrative purposes.
3. Space should be available for the student's name, the name and section of the class, the date, and any other information the teacher may want.
4. Adequate space must be provided for the kind of answers called for in the questions.
5. The breaks between pages should not be confusing.
6. The test should be economical to reproduce, assemble, and distribute.
7. There should be a variety of kinds of questions—multiple choice, true-false, essay items—to cut across students' strengths and weaknesses. Some students have great trouble with certain kinds of questions.

Subject-content:

1. Ambiguous and disputable topics should not appear, for credit, on the test.
2. Each question should stand alone.

3. Avoid specific determiners—always, never, all, every, none, each—for they make the question disputable.
4. Avoid testing on the minutiae of the course.
5. Do not test the same material over and over in different questions.
6. Avoid questions with obvious answers.
7. The individual items should proceed from easy to difficult.
8. An "average C student" should be able to complete the test without nervous exhaustion.
9. The test must be valid from the standpoint of its coverage of the announced subject of the course. Stick to the subject.
10. The test results should be compatible with the objectives of the course.

Grading Procedures:

1. Grading should be sufficiently objective so that several well-qualified people could grade it.
2. Correct responses should not follow a pattern.
3. Grading should be quantified in arabic units. The numerical grade can then be converted to a letter grade, if such is wanted.
4. The various questions should be marked according to their value or weight so that the student knows where to spend his time most profitably.

Aside from these general principles of test construction, there are a few considerations to be observed in the various specific forms of test questions. At least six forms are common.

True-False Form:

1. Use a capital T and a capital F, and have the students encircle the correct response.
2. Keep the length uniform. Long items are usually true.
3. Construct items that are entirely true or entirely false.
4. Avoid double negatives.

Multiple Choice Form:

1. Have a consistent number of choices, perhaps four or five for each item.
2. Make all choices plausible. A humorous item is fun, but it reduces the validity of the question.
3. Make all choices roughly equal in length, for unduly long ones are likely to be correct.

Completion Form:

1. Make all blanks the same length without regard to the length of the answer wanted.

2. Give enough information so that only one answer is possible.
3. Avoid beginning with a blank.
4. Use only one blank per question.

Matching Form:

1. Have more answers than terms.
2. Be consistent with the terms. Make them all nouns, or verbals, or phrases, etc.
3. Ask for only one answer—the best answer—for each term.

Short-Answer Form:

1. Specify whether or not sentences or sentence fragments are acceptable.
2. Give precise information that triggers a precise response.

Essay Form:

1. Give enough information so that no confusion exists on the kind of essay to be written.
2. Specify whether or not outlines, diagrams, and other time-saving devices will be permitted.

CALCULATING GRADES FOR STUDENTS IN PERFORMING GROUPS

Arriving at grades for the members of a performing group is one of the most difficult tasks to confront a new music director. He probably has three hundred to four hundred youngsters under his guidance in three or four different performing ensembles, and he feels, with some justification, that he cannot take the time to construct, administer, and grade quizzes and assigned papers. And in the absence of these academic procedures he frequently settles into a system of grading on attendance. Perfect attendance earns an "A"; less than perfect attendance, something lower. This basis for grading is sometimes modified to allow for class behavior to enter the calculation. Thus, a student might have perfect attendance, but get something less than an "A" because of his lethargy, or bothersome talking, or general rudeness, or whatever.

Band directors sometimes develop rather militaristic point systems, with a specific number of points awarded for attendance, "checking off" music before contests and festivals, uniform and instrument inspections, and similar clearly defined obligations. Points are deducted for tardiness, broken reeds, lost music, chewing gum, and the like. The six-weeks grade is, then, merely a matter determining the student's total as compared with the total possible. The director sets the boundaries of the letter categories, and the student accepts his fate because he has had quite a hand in determining that fate.

As a general rule, choir directors and orchestra directors do not feel comfortable with a rigid point system. They will often modify it considerably. Or they may just distribute grades on a completely subjective basis. The lack of objective and quantified scores does not work ill nearly as much as an outsider might predict. The director is really considering many factors—attitude, performance ability, attendance, and similar concrete factors. He is just not putting these items on paper, assigning numerical weight to them, and calculating the grades therefrom.

Each director will have to work out a system for himself, taking into consideration the school policies, the sizes of his performing groups, the number and reliability of his student assistants, and all manner of variables. Certainly two factors should prevail in any system to be developed: (1) the student's performance in relation to his native potential for performance, and (2) the student's contribution to the general social stability for the group—attitude, attendance, cooperation, ambition, and the like.

CHAPTER 10

Professional Growth and Development

Chapter 9 dealt with the music educator's tools, techniques, and materials for determining the musical capacity and achievement of his pupils. This is only half the job. The other half of the job is for the music educator to strive, continually, to upgrade instructional tools, techniques, and materials for his own professional growth and development. Three large areas of concern are extremely important: (1) printed reference materials, (2) clinics, workshops, and conferences, and (3) advanced study.

PRINTED REFERENCE MATERIALS

Beginning music teachers often lament that they must spend so much time searching for good music. The following materials are recommended as standard reference items in the music teacher's professional library.

Repertory Manuals

1. *Selective Music Lists: Instrumental and Vocal Solos, Instrumental and Vocal Ensembles.* Prepared by the National Interscholastic Music Activities Commission, Arthur G. Harrell, Chairman of the Music Selection Committee. Washington, D.C.: Music Educators National Conference, 1966. 160 pp., $2.00.

This manual lists hundreds of compositions for all manner of instrumental and vocal solos and ensembles. Unusual combinations (two clarinets and bassoon [16 titles], for example) are given with the standard fare (woodwind quintet [176 titles]). The compositions are for the most part by recognized first-rate composers, frequently by the giants in the field, Beethoven, Mozart, Bach, Brahms, and others. The compositions are graded in three large areas, each subdivided into two smaller areas: Easy—Grades I and II (Elementary School); Medium—Grades III and IV (Junior and Senior High School); Difficult—Grades V and VI (Senior High School and College).

2. *Selective Music Lists: Choral, String Orchestra, Orchestra, and Band.* Prepared by the National Interscholastic Music Activities Commission, Arthur G. Harrell, Chairman of the Music Selection Committee. Washington, D.C.: Music Educators National Conference, 1964. 96 pp., $2.00.

This manual lists hundreds of compositions for large and small bands, orchestras, and choral groups. The compositions for choral groups are listed by general class (Sacred, Secular, and Spirituals) and by voice assignments (SA, or SSA, or SATB, etc.). Major choral work, cantatas and oratorios, are given with separate listings for women's voices, for men's voices, for SAB, and for SATB. The compositions are graded in three large areas, each subdivided into two smaller areas: Easy—Grades I and II (Class C and D groups); Medium—Grades III and IV (Class B and C groups); Difficult—Grades V and VI (Class A and B groups).

3. *Materials for Miscellaneous Instrumental Ensembles.* Prepared by the Committee on Literature and Interpretation of Music for Instrumental Ensembles, George E. Waln, Chairman. Washington, D.C.: Music Educators National Conference, 1960. 90 pp., $2.00.

This manual lists, by large area (Strings, Woodwinds, Brasswinds, and Percussion) and grade (I-VI [Elementary School through College]), hundreds of titles for the standard and the unusual collections of instruments. Each large class is arranged from small to large groups within the class, and each group thereunder is listed alphabetically by composer.

4. *Contemporary Music: A Suggested List for High Schools and Colleges.* Prepared by the Committee on Contemporary Music, George Howerton, Chairman. Washington, D.C.: Music Educators National Conference, 1964. 32 pp., $1.00.

This manual lists, in five large categories (Original Compositions for Band, Transcriptions for Band, Orchestra, String Orchestra, and Vocal Music [Mixed Voices, Female Voices, and Male Voices]) and at three levels (Easy—for average school groups [not beginners]; Medium—requiring a rather high level of performance; and difficult—requiring the highest level of performance, equivalent to that of the best high school and college organizations), hundreds of compositions written in twentieth-century style.

5. *Contemporary Music for Schools: A Catalog of Works Written by Composers Participating in the Young Composers Projects, 1959–1964.* Sponsored by the Ford Foundation and the National Music Council. Published jointly by the Contemporary Music Project for Creativity in Music Education and the Music Educators National Conference. Norman Dello Joio is chairman of the Project, Grant Beglarian is Director. Washington, D.C.: CMP and MENC, 1966. 88 pp., $1.00.

This manual lists, by large areas (Chorus, Band, Orchestra, and Ensemble) and alphabetically thereunder, 575 compositions by thirty-nine young composers who have worked in residence in forty-four different school systems. A good number of the compositions have been published, and some are available for rental. Information of the availability of all of the compositions is easily determined by writing to the Music Educators National Conference.

6. *Original Manuscript Music for Wind and Percussion Instruments.* Compiled by Richard K. Weerts, Manuscript Music Editor for the National Association of College Wind and Percussion Instructors, an associated organization of the Music Educators National Conference. Washington, D.C.: Music Educators National Conference, 1964. 52 pp., $1.25.

More than 400 titles are listed for original compositions for wind and percussion instruments by American composers and twenty-seven titles of arrangements from other media for winds and percussion.

7. *A Selective List of Choral and Vocal Music with Wind and Percussion Accompaniments.* Prepared by Robert Vagner. Washington, D.C.: Music Educators National Conference, 1966. 13 pp., $0.50.

Included are many, many titles for mixed choral groups, men's choral groups, women's choral groups, solo voice settings, and children's choral groups—each with winds-and-percussion accompaniment.

8. Each publishing house has a catalog of its available titles. A music teacher should set aside a complete drawer in his filing cabinet for such catalogs, filed alphabetically by publishers' names. A short letter to the publishing companies will bring a flood of catalogs and publicity releases to the teacher's desk.

The above manuals are the result of years of careful examination and selection, by distinguished professional music educators, of the very best in high-quality music within the technical capabilities of public school musicians. For $9.75, a beginning music teacher can have the entire collection of manuals at his fingertips for quick reference.

Repertory Lists in Textbooks

Several textbooks have extensive sections which offer a wealth of specific information on instructional materials.

1. Karl D. Ernst and Charles L. Gary (eds.), *Music in General Education*. Washington, D.C.: Music Educators National Conference, 1965.

The book is organized around content areas—Elements of Music, Form and Design in Music, Interpretive Aspects of Music, etc. At the end of topics and subtopics within the content areas there are listed many specific works which lend themselves to clarifying and reinforcing the concepts under examination.

2. William R. Sur and Charles F. Schuller, *Music Education for Teen-Agers*, 2nd ed. New York: Harper & Row, Publishers, 1966.

Part II, "The Music Educator's Reference File," is nearly a complete manual in itself. Hundreds upon hundreds of books, films and recordings, musical compositions, audiovisual materials and equipment sources, and sources of literature and music equipment and supplies are listed with all the information needed to acquire the same.

3. Dated, but still one of the most interesting, authoritative, and comprehensive statements in the field is Peter W. Dykema and Karl W. Gehrkens, *The Teaching and Administration of High School Music*. Boston: C. C. Birchard and Co., 1941.

See Appendices C, E, J, and K for lists of traditional, substantial music for all media. Much of this music is still available.

4. Robert L. Garretson, *Conducting Choral Music*, 2nd ed. Boston: Allyn and Bacon, Inc., 1965.

The Appendix, "Source Information," contains extensive lists of compositions for choral groups and lists of related items of concern to the director of choral music.

Periodicals

There is no better way to stay abreast of the field than to follow the thinking of the profession-at-large and its subgroups in the various journals so readily available.

1. The official organ of the music education profession is the *Music Educators Journal*, edited by Charles R. Fowler. The magazine is published nine times each year (monthly, except June, July, and August),

and it contains all important announcements, projects, meetings, advertisements of new equipment and materials, book reviews, and related information of general and special interest. Feature articles by MENC members and by distinguished guests provide a solid body of stimulating reading in each issue.

2. Journals of federated state units of the Music Educators National Conference serve their respective states in the same manner as the *MEJ* serves the nation. Contest lists, lists of adjudicators, and similar information of regional interest make these publications most important reading for music educators in each state.

3. The *International Music Educator*, edited by Egon Kraus. This semiannual journal is the official organ of the International Society for Music Education (ISME). The ISME meets every other year and is rapidly becoming important in the scope of its concern and involvement in music education systems throughout the Western world. It contains no advertisements, only selected speeches from ISME conferences—each speech being printed in English, in French, and in German.

4. The *Journal of Research in Music Education*, edited by Allen P. Britton. This publication of the Society for Research in Music Education of the Music Educators National Conference is published quarterly by the MENC. The journal carries summary papers of the most elaborate and rigorous researches of the members of the profession. Book reviews and important announcements to scholars and researchers in the field are contained in the back of each number.

5. The *Bulletin of the Council for Research in Music Education*, edited by Richard J. Cowell. Published semiannually by the School of Music, University of Illinois, and the Illinois Office of the Superintendent of Public Instruction, this journal carries summary papers of selected research of members of the profession and reviews of dissertations in music and in closely related disciplines.

6. *The Choral Journal*, R. Wayne Hugoboom, Managing Editor. This journal is the official publication of the American Choral Directors Association, and it appears six times each year. Articles, news items, announcements, advertisements, and related information make up the bulk of the magazine.

7. *The Instrumentalist*, edited by John Christie. Published monthly (except July), this magazine leans a bit toward things of special interest to band directors.

8. *The American String Teacher*, edited by Paul Askegaard. This quarterly speaks to the special needs of the members of the American String Teachers Association.

It is no coincidence that the most aggressive, imaginative, and productive members of the profession read these professional journals with careful attention. Experienced teachers may find the articles a bit repetitive, occasionally, but beginning teachers will find a wealth of specific, functional information to aid them in the development of their teaching skills.

CLINICS, WORKSHOPS, AND CONFERENCES

For all that is written and spoken about teaching, there is simply no way to describe the real sensation to someone who has never taught. No amount of study and reflection on the art of teaching can equal a mere five minutes of actual teaching. And after five minutes of actual teaching, all forms of study and reflection on the art of teaching take on a new significance.

Everyone teaches, informally, all the time. Fathers and mothers teach their youngsters, neighbors teach each other the unwritten code of the neighborhood, secretaries teach each other office procedures. But to teach in a formal setting, within an authorized institutional, traditional frame of reference, with students and parents expecting demonstrable evidence of achievement, with educational administrators and community leaders looking for clear-cut signs of professional competence and style, with teaching colleagues making daily judgments and appraisals, with the uneasy feeling that the lessons are adequate, but not compelling, dynamic, and all that the methods books have said lessons ought to be—this is a completely unique experience.

Unique and brief. Ever so brief for, strangely enough, a teacher very quickly falls into a fairly secure and comfortable professional manner. The enormous ego-investment which each music teacher has in his work precludes any kind of extended period of experimentation and indecision. His superego will simply not permit him to teach very long without the crystallization of certain mannerisms and techniques. Teaching music is so intellectually complex and so emotionally all-consuming that serious psychosomatic disturbances would soon develop if a teacher were to try to carefully think through each instructional gesture, each lesson, each period, each day. The exhilarating sense of purpose and involvement sustains a music teacher through the first year or two, and gives him seemingly unlimited energy and creative vitality. The novelty soon wears off, though, and he finds that the job has its routine tasks and its predictable problems. By the end of the third year, the typical music educator will have developed a complete set of methodological techniques for dealing with nearly all phases of the instructional program.

Frequently—and this is a perfectly good procedure—the beginning teacher will have "tried on" several personalities. He will have copied, consciously or unconsciously, the mannerisms of one or more of his own favorite teachers. The results are often quite satisfactory as a temporary pretense. Indeed, asking "What would Dr. Smith have done in this case?" will give a beginning teacher a workable, ready-made solution to an especially perplexing problem. It matters not if Dr. Smith would really have taken the action taken by the beginning teacher; the act of thinking through the problem from the standpoint of an outsider brings a certain detachment and objectivity to the situation. The technique of "pretending" is informative and professionally enlightening.

Pretending to be someone else is temporary, artificial, and, in the long run, emotionally fatiguing and self-defeating. Sooner or later the teacher must come to terms with himself. At about the end of his third year of teaching, he is ready. He now needs to break loose—to start again, to change the patterns, to stop copying others, to reexamine his own peculiar talent for teaching, to modify his crystallized theories, to take a really detached look at his unfolding professional career.

He was not earlier in a position to take a detached look at himself. He was too engrossed in searching for himself. He had too many things to straighten out in his life. He had too many debts to pay, too many personal relationships to work out—marriage, children, living conditions, social adjustments, and so forth. He was too busy learning the role of music educator in its socioeconomic setting. He is ready now, though, to take an accurate inventory of his unique potential, ready to bring real substance to his professional aspirations.

The most direct and immediate manner of taking an inventory of professional stock is to start to attend the many clinics, workshops, and conferences of the profession. These professional gatherings will make a lot more sense to the young music teacher now than they would have in the first few days of his career.

First, he will be exposed to a wealth of specific information on how to improve himself in the very job he aspires so earnestly to do well. Second, he will acquire a sense of belonging to a cause larger than his own immediate cause. Third, he will begin to see himself in proper perspective.

He will observe distinguished master teachers and performers demonstrate the qualities that have made them distinguished master teachers and performers. He will hear formal and informal remarks on all aspects of his professional commitment. He will be pleasantly surprised to learn that his compatriots suffer the same misgivings as he, that they drive toward the same goals as he, that they are going through the same kind of perplexing growth traumata.

He will hear stunning performances that will inspire him to revitalized effort with his own groups. He will hear mediocre performances that will give him a quiet sense of confidence in his own work. He will gradually develop a feeling for his own special interests and competencies. He will, in short, become a member of the profession-at-large.

To be a member of the profession-at-large requires this expenditure of time, energy, and money. Young teachers often resist active involvement in their profession on purely financial grounds. Travel expenses, hotel bills, registration fees, food costs, membership dues, and subscription charges amount to a seemingly unjustified financial burden; thus, young teachers often procrastinate and find various reasons for not getting involved in all these activities of their colleagues. This is a grave error.

The financial requirements should be looked upon as necessary items in the personal budget. It simply makes no sense at all to spend thousands of dollars in preparation for a professional career, and then refuse to take part in the full responsibilities and rewards of that professional career. On the one hand, attendance at professional gatherings will keep a music teacher fully aware of new positions opening around him. If he aspires to a better job, with better working facilities in a larger school and with more talented youngsters, he will learn of these opportunities at the conferences and conventions. On the other hand, a music teacher may well learn that his present position is rather good compared to the limitations of some of his colleagues' positions. In either case, this is the kind of information a new teacher should seek out as he builds his career in the field.

Building a career in a chosen field is, incidentally, a perfectly proper professional concern. A music educator is as entitled to seek promotions, salary increases, and better working conditions as is a business executive, a career diplomat, or a corporation lawyer. A move to a new job at a better salary gives a music teacher an ego-building sense of achievement, to be sure, and this brings to him a certain status and financial security. Equally important, though, a move to a better job forces a music teacher into new responsibilities and more demanding standards of professional productivity. The result is nearly always good for the individual and the profession-at-large.

As he matures, a music teacher's competency increases. As his competency increases, his standards and goals are raised. This cause-and-effect pattern moves along until he reaches what might be called a professional plateau. At this point—the end of the fifth or sixth year, perhaps —he has brought his pedagogical talents up to his musical talents. He is about as efficient and effective as he is going to get. Two possibilities present themselves.

One, the music teacher may settle back to repeat his first five years of experience over and over again, either in the same school or in different schools of the same size and potential. If by nature he is restless, he moves every five or six years, seeking, each time, unconsciously, a situation that will provide the challenge he knows he can meet. If by nature he is not restless, he stays in the same school system, repeating a predictable cycle of challenge-and-success with each year's new group of beginners. There is nothing at all wrong with either of these career patterns. Solid and respectable contributions are being made to the goals of the music education profession. The point is—and each teacher must decide this for himself—he may not be working up to his full potential.

Two, the music teacher may decide to push himself, to enlarge his potential, to return to college for further training.

ADVANCED STUDY

The need for advanced study—or to put it another way, the possibility of a kind of repetitive pattern—is so universally recognized that school officials, working through state certification laws, demand evidence of advanced study, in addition to successful teaching experience, before they grant permanent certificates to practitioners in the field.

State certification boards are quite justified in this requirement. The law is good. The spirit and intent of the law shows real insight into the problem of bringing continual improvement to public music instruction. A grave misunderstanding has somehow developed, however, in the common manner of meeting this legal requirement.

The grave misunderstanding is simply this. "Evidence of advanced study" is freely and erroneously interpreted as evidence of advanced study in the methodology of the trade, indeed, as evidence of advanced study in nearly any area that even remotely pertains to public education. In-service music educators return to the college campus and ask for—and state certification boards permit, and departments of music education provide—a wide variety of seminars, practicums, *ad interim* projects, curriculum discussion groups, and all manner of advanced principles and practices of the trade. The results are often disappointing and misleading.

They are disappointing because the successful teacher-in-service has already found working solutions to the eternal problems of discipline, motivation, curriculum scope and sequence, audiovisual aids, evaluation and measurement, school-community relations, group dynamics, and the other classic educational concerns. He has already developed a working professional manner based on his own set of individual strengths and weaknesses. Chances are small that his classmates' discussion will change his approach to his own school-and-community environment. Chances are also small that the force and immediacy of his own experience will be altered very much by the prepared lectures of the college professor. It is not uncommon at all for graduate music education students to find that a good portion of their graduate studies bears an uncomfortable resemblance to the very same kind of discussions that go on in their teachers' lounge in their home school.

The results are misleading because the music teacher-in-service gets graduate credit for what is not really advanced study in the discipline of his profession. He gets graduate credit for engaging in the collective act of reexamining, reevaluating, and reaffirming his own unique, professional trade skills. He may read a series of stimulating articles, and write several extended papers, and examine the latest instructional materials, and review the most recent textbooks, and witness stunning demonstrations of the newest audiovisual equipment, but he often returns to the classroom the same musician he was when he began his graduate studies.

He should not. He should return to the classroom a different, a more knowledgeable, a more sophisticated musician. However time-consuming and uncomfortable it may be, he should seek out the kind of graduate studies that force him to probe deeper into the substance of his profession—into music, as such. Extended dialogue and discussion about the daily operations of the profession will not bring him to increased knowledgeability and sophistication as a musician. And it is only as his command of the art of music expands that his real potential as a music teacher expands.

The music educator does not need advanced study in individual differences among public school musicians, or in the school and its relevance to contemporary society, or in the limitations of adolescent skills in performance, or in formal educational theory. These differences, relevance, and limitations he witnesses around him all day long, and he labors daily in educational operations that have not yet been crystallized into formal educational theory. Rather, he needs advanced study in differences of musical styles—historical differences, idiomatic differences, differences in aesthetic intent. He needs advanced study in contemporary music and its relevance to twentieth-century information media, in applied music to reduce the limitations of his own skills in performance, and he needs advanced study in music theory. He returns to his work, then, an enlarged musician.

If he returns to his work with increased insight into the art of music and with reaffirmed confidence in his own musical competence, a music educator stands at the threshold of new experiences in his professional growth and development, and this leads, nearly always, to new and exciting experiences in musical perception and understanding for his students, for the school system, and for the community-at-large. This is, after all, the whole purpose for advanced professional study.

CONCLUSION

This brings Chapter 10 and the textbook to a close. It has been the intent of this book to present what seem to be the most promising avenues of professional thought and action for music educators. The avenues are extremely wide, and the center lines are not always clearly defined. Weather conditions are variable and unpredictable, and the surrounding land is often new and strange.

The music education student will soon travel along these avenues—under his own power, in a vehicle of his own unique design, at his own proper rate of speed. It is earnestly hoped that this textbook will give a sense of direction and purpose to the journey.

Annotated Bibliography

AMERICAN EDUCATIONAL RESEARCH ASSOCIATION. *Education Programs: Adolescence.* Being the *Review of Educational Research*, XXXVI, No. 4 (October 1966). Washington, D.C.: American Educational Research Association, 1966.

Reviews the literature for the six-year period since the issuance of XXX, No. 1 (February 1960). Summarizes, in brilliant essays, the most rigorous thinking on adolescent behavior, cultural deprivation, and cognitive development. Seven discussions; extensive bibliography for each; index for the entire manual. David P. Ausubel served as chairman for the Association's committee on this project.

AUSUBEL, DAVID P. See American Educational Research Association.

BIENSTOCK, SYLVIA F. See Jersild, Arthur T.

BRITTON, ALLEN P. "Music Education: An American Specialty," in *One Hundred Years of Music in America*, Paul Henry Lang (ed.). New York: G. Schirmer, Inc., 1961.

Reprinted in *Music Educators Journal* (XLVIII, No. 6 [June–July 1962]) and in *Perspectives in Music Education* (MENC Source Book III), edited by Bonnie C. Kowall. One of the most penetrating examinations in print of the central conditions of the music education profession and its development as a peculiarly American phenomenon.

CHIDESTER, LAWRENCE W. See Prescott, Gerald R.

COLE, LUELLA. *Psychology of Adolescence*, 5th ed. New York: Holt, Rinehart and Winston, Inc., 1959.

A leading textbook in the field. The bibliographies at the ends of the chapters cover a wide range of somewhat dated, but pointedly relevant, reference sources.

COLEMAN, JAMES S. *The Adolescent Society*. New York: Free Press of Glencoe, 1961.

A stimulating and enlightening exploration of adolescent mores, aspirations, systems of value, and reference groups. Important reading for all who hope to work in public education at the level of the secondary school.

COOPER, IRVIN. *Letters to Pat Concerning Junior High School Vocal Problems.* New York: Carl Fischer, Inc., 1953.

An interesting and informative delivery of the author's theories and principles. Recommended for general-music specialists.

————, and KARL O. KUERSTEINER. *Teaching Junior High School Music: General Music and the Vocal Program.* Boston: Allyn and Bacon, Inc., 1965.

The result of twenty years of diligent work in the area of junior high school vocal music. The controversial nature of Cooper's "cambiata"— "the boy's voice passing through the first change" (p. 15)—sometimes beclouds the man and his labor. All factors considered, this textbook explores the choral approach to the general music class with remarkable precision and clarity.

DUVAL, W. CLYDE. *The High School Band Director's Handbook.* Englewood Cliffs, N.J.: Prentice-Hall, Inc., 1960.

Solid techniques drawn from many years of experience. Concise, well written, carefully organized.

DYKEMA, PETER W., and KARL W. GEHRKENS. *The Teaching and Administration of High School Music.* Boston: C. C. Birchard and Co., 1940.

A classic treatment of the announced subject. Nearly all of the topics under careful discussion today have been examined here—piano classes, the dance band, chamber music, etc. Very well written, sources carefully documented, opinions and observations still accurate and valid.

ERNST, KARL D., and CHARLES L. GARY (eds.). *Music in General Education.* Washington, D. C.: Music Educators National Conference, 1965.

A remarkably informative and stimulating presentation of what the sum and substance of music instruction ought to be in the common schooling of the children of the nation. Speaks to all issues in the task. Conceived and delivered with assuredness and style. An extremely important manual.

GARRETSON, ROBERT L. *Conducting Choral Music,* 2nd ed. Boston: Allyn and Bacon, Inc., 1965.

Complete coverage of all important aspects of the announced subject. The appendix, "Source Information," contains a wealth of specific, useful information.

GARY, CHARLES L. (co-ed.). *Music in General Education.* See Ernst, Karl D.

GEHRKENS, KARL W. See Dykema, Peter W.

GIDDINGS, THADDEUS P. See Maddy, Joseph E.

GREEN, ELIZABETH A. H. *The Modern Conductor.* Englewood Cliffs, N.J.: Prentice-Hall, Inc., 1961.

A comprehensive treatise on the conductors' technique—in the full sense of the term *technique*. Chapter 18, "The Melded Gestures and Psychological Conducting," for example, is a unique and imaginative discussion of an important set of concepts and procedures.

HAYNIE, WILLIAM S. See Leeder, Joseph A.

HENDRICKSON, GORDON. "Music," in *Encyclopedia of Educational Research*, 3rd ed., Chester W. Harris (ed.). New York: Macmillan Co., 1960.

A compilation, review, and evaluation of research in music and in music education. Recommended highly for its complete and concise coverage of the field to 1960.

HENRY, NELSON B. (ed.). *Basic Concepts in Music Education*. The Fifty-seventh Yearbook of the National Society for the Study of Education. Chicago: The University of Chicago Press, 1958.

Fourteen distinguished authorities in education, philosophy, sociology, psychology, and music education reflect on the announced subject. A required purchase in nearly every graduate music education program in the nation.

HILGARD, ERNEST R. *Theories of Learning*, 2nd ed. New York: Appleton-Century-Crofts, Inc., 1956.

A comprehensive and discerning examination of the complexities of human learning. One of the classic treatises in the field.

HOFFER, CHARLES R. *Teaching Music in the Secondary Schools*. Belmont, Calif.: Wadsworth Publishing Co., Inc., 1964.

One of the most complete and interestingly written textbooks in the field. Sources documented, opinions and observations carefully and fully developed.

HOUSE, ROBERT W. See Leonhard, Charles.

————. *Instrumental Music for Today's Schools*. Englewood Cliffs, N.J.: Prentice-Hall, Inc., 1965.

A full treatment of the announced subject. Well written, carefully organized.

HORNER, V. *Music Education: The Background of Research and Opinion*. Hawthorn, Victoria, Australia: Australian Council for Educational Research, 1965.

An admirable attempt to review and evaluate a large body of information derived from research studies and personal experiences. Deals mostly with works written in English. Recommended highly for a general survey of the field, and for bibliographic leads into areas of special interest.

JERSILD, ARTHUR T., and SYLVIA F. BIENSTOCK. "A Study of the Development of Children's Ability to Sing." *Journal of Educational Psychology*, XXV, No. 7 (1934).

Dated, but still holds up. See Horner, *op. cit.*, pp. 115–16.

KAPLAN, MAX. *Foundations and Frontiers of Music Education.* New York: Holt, Rinehart and Winston, Inc., 1966.

A major contribution to the growing literature on the sociology of music education. Digs below the surface of the music education profession to examine hundreds of topics on which rigorous, full-blown research is needed. Like Merriam in *The Anthropology of Music*, Kaplan asks a lot of uncomfortable questions. The narrative is organized and well written. All is thoroughly documented. An extremely important work.

KOWALL, BONNIE C. (ed.). *Perspectives in Music Education: Source Book III.* Washington, D. C.: Music Educators National Conference, 1966.

Recent articles by eighty-four authors, culled from thirty-one publications, on issues important to the profession. The selections have been arranged to show conflicting views on various topics. All in all, a splendid compilation.

KUERSTEINER, KARL O. See Cooper, Irvin.

KUHN, WOLFGANG E. *Instrumental Music: Principles and Methods of Instruction.* Boston: Allyn and Bacon, Inc., 1962.

A refreshingly compact, yet full and systematic, presentation of all aspects of the instrumental music teacher's professional needs. Chapter 6, "Planning the Rehearsal," is especially well done.

LEEDER, JOSEPH A., and WILLIAM S. HAYNIE. *Music Education in the High School.* Englewood Cliffs, N.J.: Prentice-Hall, Inc., 1958.

In its eighth printing and still informative. A comprehensive textbook dealing with all dimensions of secondary school music instruction. Lists repertories and materials wherever appropriate at the end of the units.

LEONHARD, CHARLES, and ROBERT W. HOUSE. *Foundations and Principles of Music Education.* New York: McGraw-Hill Book Co., Inc., 1959.

An examination of the philosophical, psychological, and historical bases for music education, and the presentation of guiding principles deriving therefrom.

MADDY, JOSEPH E., and THADDEUS P. GIDDINGS. *Instrumental Technique for Orchestra and Band.* Cincinnati: The Willis Music Co., 1926.

Nothing has been written since its appearance to invalidate one single word of this magnificent textbook. The authors' complete grasp of the subject, and their insight into the psychological needs and social aspirations of adolescent instrumentalists, is as stimulating to read today as it must have been forty-two years ago. This is no rare-book display item. It is profitable reading, every page. A remarkable treatise.

MERRIAM, ALAN P. *The Anthropology of Music.* Evanston, Ill.: Northwestern University Press, 1964.

A cross-cultural look at music as a form of human behavior. Serious questions, by the score, are raised—questions to which scholars in all branches of the music profession must soon address themselves. The sections on music teaching and music learning are disturbing to read.

Merriam demonstrates, with uncomfortable regularity, how little is really known about teaching and learning music. Hundreds of seeds for imaginative and significant research in music education are scattered in these pages. The most thought-provoking treatise to appear in quite some time. Fully documented, written in a sometimes uneven but scholarly manner, develops its points with consistent precision.

NORMANN, THEODORE F. *Instrumental Music in the Public Schools.* Philadelphia: Oliver Ditson Co., 1939.

This textbook, like Prescott and Chidester, *Getting Results,* served to bring things into focus for an entire generation of band directors in the 1940's and early 1950's. It is still profitable reading.

PRESCOTT, GERALD R., and LAWRENCE W. CHIDESTER. *Getting Results with School Bands.* Minneapolis: Paul A. Schmitt Music Co., 1938.

A rigorous and systematic approach to the public school band and its successful development. A large number of currently efficient and effective band directors grew up with this textbook as a constant source of information and inspiration.

RUDOLF, MAX. *The Grammar of Conducting: A Practical Study of Modern Baton Technique.* Foreword by George Szell. New York: G. Schirmer, Inc., 1950.

A classic—indeed, the definitive—treatment of the announced subject. The examples are many, and the narrative is a model of forthright clarity. Each page will bear rich dividends to the serious student.

SCHULLER, CHARLES F. See Sur, William R.

SINGLETON, IRA C. *Music in Secondary Schools.* Boston: Allyn and Bacon, Inc., 1963.

The original edition of the present work. In the interest of brevity, the present edition has compressed and revised large sections of the original.

SUR, WILLIAM R., and CHARLES F. SCHULLER. *Music Education for Teen-Agers,* 2nd ed. New York: Harper & Row, Publishers, 1966.

One of the publisher's Exploration Series in Education, under the advisory editorship of John Guy Fowlkes. Part II, "The Music Educator's Reference File," is a comprehensive compilation of audiovisual materials, equipment suppliers, specific musical compositions for all media, etc.

WALLER, GILBERT (Chairman, MENC Committee on String Instruction in the Schools). *String Instruction Program.* Washington, D. C.: Music Educators National Conference, 1957.

Under Waller's distinguished leadership, ten manuals on important aspects of string instruction have been assembled. Each manual was prepared by an experienced authority working with a subcommittee. A most commendable series.

Index